CITYSPOTS
COPEN

Pat Levy

Written by Pat Levy
Original photography and research by Pat Levy
Front cover photography courtesy of Alamy Images

Produced by 183 Books
Design/layout/maps: Chris Lane and Lee Biggadike
Editorial/project management: Stephen York

Published by Thomas Cook Publishing
A division of Thomas Cook Tour Operations Limited
PO Box 227, Units 15/16, Coningsby Road
Peterborough PE3 8SB, United Kingdom
email: books@thomascook.com
www.thomascookpublishing.com
+44 (0)1733 416477

First edition © 2006 Thomas Cook Publishing
Text © 2006 Thomas Cook Publishing
Maps © 2006 Thomas Cook Publishing
ISBN-13: 978-1-84157-584-1
ISBN-10: 1-84157-584-4
Project Editor: Kelly Anne Pipes
Production/DTP: Steven Collins

Although every care has been taken in compiling this publication, and the contents are believed to be correct at the time of printing, Thomas Cook Tour Operations Limited cannot accept any responsibility for errors or omissions, however caused, or for changes in details given in this book, or for the consequences of any reliance on the information provided. Descriptions and assessments are based on the author's views and experiences at time of writing and do not necessarily represent those of Thomas Cook Tour Operations Limited.

Printed and bound in Spain by GraphyCems

CONTENTS

SYMBOLS & ABBREVIATIONS

The following symbols are used throughout this book:

- ☎ telephone   ⚡ fax   ⓔ email   ⓦ website address
- ⓐ address   ⓛ opening times   ⓝ public transport connections

The following symbols are used on the maps:

- 🅸   Tourist Information Office
- ✈   Airport

Hotels and restaurants are graded by approximate price as follows:
K budget   **KK** mid-range   **KKK** expensive   **KKK+** luxury

24-HOUR CLOCK

All times in this book are given in the 24-hour clock system used widely in Europe and in most international transport timetables.

▶ *The Marmorkirke – built as Copenhagen's answer to Rome's St Peter's*

Introduction

Small but perfectly formed, Copenhagen is the ideal city to visit, whether for a few days or a fortnight, in summer or winter. It's so small you could be talking about it like an old hand within a day or so, yet so complex and rich with things to see and do that you could stay a fortnight and just scratch the surface. A car is the least necessary thing in this city, where you can walk from one area to another in half an hour and where a shiny new metro system is opening up further reaches of the city even as you read.

Pedestrianised streets and wide, ancient city squares mean that in summer, and well into the autumn, the pavements are places to relax, not dodge the traffic. Culture vultures will be in art gallery heaven, thanks in large part to the city's benefactors, the royal family and the Carlsberg Foundation, while the lowbrow can let it all hang out in Tivoli or Bakken, titter at the dioramas in Museum Erotica or gawp at the royal dinner service in Rosenberg Slot.

Copenhagen is above all a happy city, comfortable with itself and its place in the world. Social unrest isn't unknown but it is purposeful and one of the strangest social experiments in Europe takes place right here in Christiania. If the city doesn't live on the cutting edge of artistic creation it certainly has some good ideas in that direction and arts buffs will find some things to amuse them, as will jazz enthusiasts, foodies, even anoraks – this place has more maritime museums and big machinery exhibits per square foot than almost anywhere else. Above all, Copenhagen has Tivoli Gardens, a public pleasure garden dedicated entirely to mindless fun, a little 21st-century Eden where all is well in the world: computer games alongside giant puppets, stomach-churning rides besides over-the-top kitsch merry-go-rounds where Hans Christian

Andersen's stories have no darker side and where your evening, like a fairy story, ends happily ever after.

🔺 *Exuberant fountains, like this one in the Nyhavn area, are a Copenhagen speciality*

When to go

British people will find Copenhagen's climate a familiar one. Perhaps a little colder and darker in winter, with longer summer days and slightly more rain than most of Britain, Copenhagen is open to visitors all year, although some of its prime sights have shorter opening hours or close completely during the winter, in particular Tivoli.

Spring, from the end of April to the middle of May, can be chilly but bright, although statistically speaking you are less likely to experience rainy days than at any other time of year. As the months move into summer and the temperature rises to a peak of around 22°C (72°F) the rainfall increases and so does humidity, but neither of them to the point where they spoil your trip. The summer sees an influx of foreign visitors while Copenhageners take their summer trips to sweaty foreign climes or the North Zealand coast. It also sees lots of festivals and events. By the end of August things start to cool down a little and mild sunny days predominate, when a cardigan or sweatshirt will be all the extra cover you need. By November it's back down to single figures on the thermometer and the temperature is often at freezing point. A good reason to visit at Christmas is the reopening of Tivoli for a month, primarily for the Christmas market.

ANNUAL EVENTS
January
New Year Celebrations in Rådhuspladsen and firework displays all over town. Lots of special concerts leading up to midnight.

February/March

Fastelavn in late Feb/early March. An ancient pagan festival where children put on fancy dress and hit a barrel until sweets fall out of it – a sort of Nordic Halloween.

Natfilm Festival in late March is 10 days of Danish and international films, shown in the original language. Including reruns, old movies and previews of as yet unreleased movies. Ⓦ www.natfilm.dk

Copenhagen Fashion and Design Festival in late March/early April has exhibitions at Nikolaj Church, special displays in shops focussing on Danish design. ❶ 33 55 74 81. Ⓦ www.nikolaj-ccac.dk

🔺 *Tivoli re-opens in April in festival mood*

Bakken Amusement Park officially opens for the year, with a parade of motorcyclists.

April/May
Queen Margarethe II's birthday (16 April). The Queen appears on the balcony at Amalienborg Slot at noon and the Royal Guard parades in ceremonial uniform.

Tivoli Gardens opens in April for the summer season

May Day Parade through the city by trade unionists to Fælled Park, where there is a rally with music events, food stalls and lots of ale.

Ølfestival (Beer festival) takes place over 3 days of May at Valby. Ⓦ www.haandbrygg.dk and www.ale.dk

Copenhagen Marathon Over 26 years old, the Copenhagen marathon circles the city on a Sunday in mid May.
Ⓦ www.copenhagenmarathon.dk

June/July
Whitsun Carnival parade from Strøget to Fælled Park. Three days of Latin American fun in Scandinavia. Ⓦ www.karneval.dk

Sankt Hans Aften 23 June is the longest day. Bonfires and parties on the beaches and in the parks.

Roskilde Festival Late June/early July. Big rock festival with 70,000 or more visitors, big names, stalls, camping, possibly mud and chemical toilets. Ⓦ www.roskilde-festival.dk

Jazz Festival July's 10 days of indoor and outdoor performances around the city (see page 12).

August/September/October
Mermaid Pride Festival Early August. Not a celebration of the statue but the annual gay pride bash. Lots of fun. Ⓦ www.mermaidpride.dk

Copenhagen Film Festival Second half of September.
Cultural Night On the first night of the school autumn term in October museums, theatres and galleries open late and are free, with free buses ferrying visitors around the venues.
ⓦ www.kulturnatten.dk

November/December
Copenhagen Autumn Jazz Four days in early November in clubs around the city. ⓦ www.jazzfestival.dk
Christmas Parade to light the tree in Rådhuspladsen on the last Saturday in November.
Tivoli Christmas market Mid November to a few days before Christmas. Ice skating, some restaurants open.

PUBLIC HOLIDAYS
Public transport runs to Sunday schedules, and banks, post offices and public buildings are closed on these days. Many shops (but not generally restaurants) will also be closed.
1 Jan New Year's Day
Mar/Apr Maundy Thursday, Good Friday & Easter Monday
Apr/May Common Prayer Day (4th Fri after Good Friday)
May Ascension Day
May/June Whit Monday
5 Jun Constitution Day
24–26 Dec Christmas holiday
31 Dec New Year's Eve

The Jazz Festival

Copenhagen's most celebrated festival takes place over 10 days in July, starting on the first Friday. It has been a local institution since it began in 1978. The peculiar popularity of jazz among Copenhagen's citizens dates back far longer – during World War II jazz became a form of resistance to the drudgery of occupation and in the 60s, as jazz fell from popularity in the USA, American jazz musicians found their way to Copenhagen, with its reputation for liberality and permissiveness. Some of them made it their home and perhaps this explains the quality and intensity of local talent and the enthusiasm and number of those happy to listen to it.

Some names that even those who know nothing about jazz will recognise – Dizzie Gillespie, Ray Charles, Ella Fitzgerald, Oscar Peterson, Winton Marsalis, the list goes on – have played here. During the jazz fortnight everywhere becomes a venue – the Cirkus Bygningen and Tivoli are where the big events predominate but cafés, parks, clubs, public squares, churches, the canal banks and the museums also form a backdrop to the hundreds of performances. The open-air events are free, cafés and clubs charge a small entrance fee and the big concerts can be expensive.

All kinds of jazz turns up here, from traditional stuff to experimental, and some of the best performances come not from the big names who line up to play here but by home-grown jazz musicians.

What is most fun about the festival is its un-Copenhagen-like qualities. You will notice that Copenhagen is normally an organised kind of place with fixed views about shop opening hours and crossing the road. The festival is so big and so decentralised that for a fortnight *hygge* (see page 16) goes out the window and a sunny, laughing chaos hits the city. In fact Copenhageners like the music and atmosphere so much they hold another festival, **Autumn Jazz**, in early November.

If you intend to visit while the festival is on it is a good idea to advance book your accommodation in this hotel-deprived city.

Copenhagen Jazz Festival ⓐ Nytorv 3. ⓣ 33 93 20 13.
ⓦ www.jazzfestival.dk

⬤ *July sees jazz all over the city – afloat, on the streets, wherever there's space*

History

Back in the 12th century Copenhagen was a scruffy hamlet called Havn, a footnote in the history of Denmark, surrounded on all sides by salt marshes and relying on fishing for trade. The dominant city was Roskilde, with its stone cathedral and kings. In 1167 King Valdemar I sent his brother Bishop Absalon to sort out pirates who were attacking shipping. Standing as it did in a strategic position to control the narrow shipping channel, the Øresund, Havn rapidly developed as Absalon built a fortress on modern Slotsholmen and set about establishing law and order.

Flash forward a couple of centuries and Köbmandshavn (merchant's port), still trading in herrings but now a strategically important location, was attacked regularly by its neighbours. In 1443 the Danish kings moved their capital to Köbmandshavn.

In 1536 there was a peasant's revolt and Copenhagen was besieged, its citizens reduced to eating rats, before surrendering to the king's forces in the same year. Christian IV began the first big building programme in the 17th century. The 18th century saw a plague which killed 20,000 people, a fire in 1728 which destroyed much of the city and a war with its neighbours lasting 30 years.

Flash forward once more to the 19th century. It started badly with another siege, this time by Admiral Lord Nelson. As the century progressed Copenhagen experienced a cultural renaissance: Hans Christian Andersen and Søren Kierkegaard lounged about the city's salons while Thorvaldsen sculpted his famous friends. The industrial revolution hit Copenhagen in the middle of the century, its citizens rapidly reduced to squalor as the population increased; Vesterbro and Nørrebro were created as workers' homes.

In 1940 Germany invaded and five years of occupation followed, during which time, Denmark, unlike any other country in Europe, rescued the vast majority of its Jews. A social welfare programme was instituted after the war and in the 1960s Denmark boomed; its first immigrants arrived to take up jobs that couldn't be filled by Danes. Copenhagen's youth joined the student protests about the bomb, Vietnam and education. The first skyscraper, the Radisson Hotel, went up, designed in its entirety by Arne Jacobsen, and pornography was legalised.

The 70s saw the establishment of the free state of Christiania in a disused army base. Denmark joined the EEC but its membership was controversial and by the 1990s it was rejecting treaties and later chose not to join the European monetary union.

In 1996 Denmark's football team won the European Cup and in 2000 the building of the Øresund Bridge linked Copenhagen with Sweden by road and rail, creating a new economic and social power. In 2005, the bicentenary of the birth of Hans Christian Andersen and the city, now dealing with immigrant communities, a right-wing government, unemployment and social unrest descended into nostalgia for a simpler time.

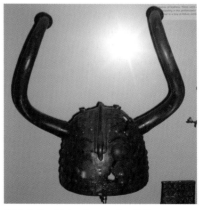

⬥ *Early Danish headgear in the National Museum*

Lifestyle

The first thing you notice in Copenhagen, after admiring the wind turbines, pretty housing estates and clean metro on your journey into town, are the pedestrian crossings. Everyone obeys them religiously and this may be a key to understanding Copenhageners. Their history hasn't been a cheerful one, what with fire, plague, siege, occupation (and not just by Germany, Sweden did some damage in earlier centuries, too) and Copenhageners, like the rest of their countrymen, like order. There is a Danish concept called *hygge*, a sort of defence mechanism whose meaning comes close to 'cosiness' or 'togetherness' and includes the idea of keeping the forces of darkness at bay with good cheer and looking after one another. Tivoli sums it up, as does the amazing social welfare system that operates in Denmark.

But if most of Copenhagen is ordered and good-natured and sensible there is anarchy in the heart of the city. Christiania is a genuinely anarchist society, run along totally democratic lines where co-operation and not the law keeps crime low and where the cannabis sellers, now long gone, kept the hard drug pushers out of the community. The community pays little or nothing in rent and taxes and looks after itself; several successful businesses are established there and lots of young people spend their weekends enjoying the atmosphere. But Christiania is prime real estate, Copenhagen's building plots are getting fewer and so Christiania's number is probably up. Go and visit an amazing, impromptu social experiment while it lasts (see pages 96–97).

SOCIAL ETIQUETTE

If you want to get on with the Danes there are a few rules to obey besides waiting till the green man is showing. Don't expect any deference from waiters or the cleaner in your hotel – everyone is equal in Copenhagen. Don't complain about other customers in the restaurant puffing smoke all over your food. It's not worth it. Keep out of the cycle lanes or you'll get a sharp 'ting' from someone's bell. Observe every British rule about queuing and then some. Danes disapprove of queue-jumping big time. (Strangely, don't expect queues at bus stops – anarchy has to have some kind of safety valve.) Don't take photographs in Christiania: it isn't the zoo.

▲ *Everyone obeys the little green man*

Culture

It is interesting that the area of culture where Denmark leads the world is interior design – *hygge*, the need to create a secure and happy environment, almost certainly feeds into that Danish talent. But Denmark has other cultural highs too, in music, literature, the theatre, the arts and cinema.

The classical music scene in Copenhagen is alive and well, if a little traditional. There are several resident classical orchestras, including the Zealand Symphony Orchestra and the Danish Radio Symphony Orchestra. Opera has received a shot in the arm with the opening in 2005 of the new opera house, with an ambitious starting programme. The city has two opera companies, which perform in the new theatre and in Den Anden Opera, where more avante garde performances take place. There is an annual opera festival at the end of May (Ⓦ www.aok.dk) and in mid-August there are free open air performances at Sondermarken.

Danish theatre, too, has its conservative and avante garde sections. For visitors the avante garde element may not be appealing, since it is largely in the medium of Danish. Det Kongelige Teater (the Royal Theatre) provides most tourist entertainment although the London Toast Theatre (Ⓦ www.londontoast.dk) provides light comedies and the like in English. Det Kongelige Teater is also the home of ballet, performed by the Danish Royal Ballet Company.

Film-making has a long history in Denmark and has been undergoing a quiet revival in recent years. In 1995 a group called Dogme was founded, led by film-maker Lars Von Trier, who has since

▶ *Humble items but great design at the Dansk Design Center*

moved on to Hollywood. Copenhagen has an international film festival in August which, although newly arrived on the film festival scene, is doing well.

But back to interior design. You will inevitably wander into one of the Danish design shops during your stay and convince yourself that you must go home, paint your walls white and get an egg chair but there is a little more to it than that. Danish furniture, cutlery and other homewares focus on an amalgam of form with function. The best of Arne Jacobsen are smooth steel teapots that don't dribble tea all over the table when you pour the tea out or cutlery that removes all unnecessary clutter from their function. The egg chair melds comfort with a simple, flowing grace (although they're annoying because you have to stand up to move them: they need rollers). An earlier chair, the 1948 Round Chair by Hans Wegner, performs a similar function of comfort with style. In the Kunstindustrimuseet (see page 68) you can see a whole history of Danish chair design. Only the Danes give their chairs names. The silversmith Georg Jensen produced beautiful silver pieces of jewellery and silverware along similar flowing lines. In modern times Danish design is thriving with shops all over town selling lovely glassware and lamps, furniture and things for the home.

❍ *Strøget is Denmark's, and Europe's, longest pedestrianised shopping street*

Shopping

WHAT TO BUY

Bargains you may not find in Copenhagen, where even the vegetables have class, but if you don't mind parting with some cash the city has lots to offer. Danish design doesn't just apply to funny-shaped chairs and bare walls; it can be found in fairly everyday items such as cutlery, pots and pans, table lamps, and even clothes. The city is full of small clothes shops with designs and sizes to suit all comers and even the vintage clothes shops somehow manage to make second-hand things look pretty smart. Good places to look for very beautiful things are the museum shops.

Purchases to look out for particularly are Arne Jacobsen-designed steel items such as his ashtray, coffee pot or vacuum flask, just the right size to get in the suitcase and not breakable. If you take care with packing, Royal Copenhagen porcelain is very collectible and there is a seconds shop in Frederiksberg if the firsts are beyond your budget. In jewellery design another Dane excels – Georg Jensen shops sell very inventive and original pieces. Amber fills the shops in great chunks but there are some pretty, delicate pieces too. Cheaper but still very desirable are the hundreds of cut-paper mobiles, many featuring events from Hans Christian Andersen stories. And if you go at the right time of year, Copenhagen sells what have to be the best Christmas decorations in Europe.

WHERE TO SHOP

Strøget and the streets leading off it are the place to start, while the pedestrianised streets of Nørrebro have lots of funky clothes, antiques and design shops. Istegade is still the place for fetish stuff,

USEFUL SHOPPING PHRASES

What time do the shops open/close?
Hvornår åbner/lukker det?
Vohnor orbna/lorka di?

How much is this?
Hvor meget koster det?
Vohr mah-eht kosta di?

I'd like to buy it.
Jeg vil gerne have det.
Yai vi gehrrneh ha di.

This is too large/too small. Do you have any others?
Den er for stor/lille. Har du andet?
Dehn ehrr fo sdoorr/leeleh. Hah doo aneht?

while Bredgade beats the lot in upmarket design and antiques.
Christiania is worth browsing around for something for your
teenage nephew and while Islands Brygge isn't yet in the big league
for really kooky design and clothes it's getting there. Copenhagen
has several weekend flea markets which are noted in the relevant
sections of the book.

SHOPPING HOURS

Shopping hours are a little antiquated in Copenhagen. Few shops
(the exception being Magasin du Nord) open on Sundays and most
only open for part of the day on Saturday. Shops generally open
around 10.00–10.30 and close between 17.00 and 18.00. Late
opening on Fridays in some of the bigger stores is until 19.00.

Eating & drinking

WHERE TO GO

Whether you just want to fill a gap, spend the evening over a beer and a good dinner or treat yourself to a luxurious six-course haute cuisine piece of culinary art, with flunkeys brushing your tablecloth, there is something for you in Copenhagen. The city has a disproportionate number of Michelin stars for its population density and there are many more very good places at the cutting edge of Danish fusion cooking.

Danish cuisine is based on seafood, especially herrings, with lots of cold climate root vegetables, dense black bread and mild cheeses, rabbit, pork and beef and lots of beer. *Smørrebrød* is an open sandwich traditionally made with rye bread or wheat bread and piled high with cold meats of one kind or another or herring and garnished with pickled vegetables or salad. In *smørrebrød* bars you can still try this traditional-style sandwich but more modern places tend to offer sandwiches with far more elaborate dressings and vegetable accompaniments.

Another traditional style of Danish restaurant fare is the buffet-style table, similar to hotel breakfasts but more heavily laden with meats and pickles and including some hot dishes. An excellent modern form of this is at Rizraz (see page 88), where a vast

RESTAURANT CATEGORIES

The following price guide, used throughout the book, indicates the average price per head for a 2–3 course dinner, excluding drinks. Lunch will usually be a little cheaper in each category.
K Below 250Kr. **KK** 250–400Kr. **KKK** Over 400Kr.

vegetarian cold table, including several hot dishes, accompanies whatever meat dish you choose.

Wienerbrød (Vienna bread), known to everyone else in the world

⬤ *Copenhagen's bar scene is young and lively*

as Danish pastries, are ubiquitous and often eaten for breakfast at a fast pace with a coffee while waiting for the train.

EATING OUT

Unless you have money to burn, eating out in Copenhagen's more expensive places is going to be a rare treat but a treat it certainly is. The most common form of cuisine in the upmarket Danish restaurants is a fusion of French and Danish, often mixing French sauces, ingredients such as *foie gras*, or cooking styles with the more basic ingredients of Danish cooking – rabbit, for example, appears on many menus, as do root vegetables and fish such as pollock, hake or mackerel. Some quite unusual things appear on your plate in the very upmarket restaurants – chickweed or nasturtium flowers wouldn't be out of place.

Fortunately for your wallet, cheaper places are also good fun and serve hearty, well cooked food. Café bars often serve hot meals all day, ethnic restaurants have taken off, especially in Nørrebro and Vesterbro and Thai restaurants, as well as the odd sushi bar, are a welcome sight in the city. Moving further downmarket you should try at least once a hot dog or burger from one of the travelling stalls parked in the squares. All over the city there are good delicatessens and supermarkets where you can buy bread, cheese, cold meats and pickles and you will inevitably be drawn by the nose to the plenitude of bakeries selling hot bread, *wienerbrød*, filled sandwiches and coffee.

DRINKING

Wine with your restaurant meal considerably adds to the final bill. Lots of people drink the more affordable beer or, with *smørrebrød*, *akvavit*, an astringent liqueur which is thrown down as quickly as possible and followed by a beer chaser.

TIPPING

A service charge is included in your bill and you rarely get a credit card receipt with a little bit at the end to add a tip. Danes don't leave elaborate tips, perhaps rounding up the bill to the nearest 10Kr or leaving 10 or 20Kr for the waiter.

USEFUL DINING PHRASES

I would like a table for ... people, please.
Et bord til ..., tak.
Id boorr ti ..., tahg.

I am a vegetarian.
Jeg er vegetar.
Yai her vehgehtar.

Where is the toilet (restroom) please?
Hvor er toilettet, tak?
Vohr ehrr toylehdeht, tahg?

May I have the bill, please?
Jeg vil gerne betale regningen.
Yai vi gehrrneh bitaleh rainingehn.

Do you accept credit cards?
Tager I kreditkort?
Tah ee krehdeedkord?

Entertainment & nightlife

Like its range of restaurants, Copenhagen's club scene has grown to match its increasing wealth and its ethnic and libertarian influences. Most musical tastes are catered to and clubs and discos exist to suit every lifestyle, wallet and age group. Many of Copenhagen's café bars metamorphose at night into clubs and lots of the clubs open during the day to serve bar food. Unlike other cities, where clubs go in and out of fashion rapidly, places such as Vega are still going strong after many years. Vega, indeed, receives government subsidies – you can't get much more respectable than that.

Clubs get going quite late especially at weekends when they are empty until well past 01.00 – possibly because drinking all night and into the early hours would be prohibitively expensive. Many clubs have a lower age limit of 21. Check out Ⓦ www.aok.dk for details of what's on.

LIVE MUSIC
Summer in Copenhagen sees many free performances of all kinds in the pedestrianised streets, the parks and churches. Major venues for classical musical performances include:

The Black Diamond (see page 95)
Christianskirke ⓐ Strandgade 2. ❶ 32 5415 76.
Ⓦ www.christianskirke.dk
Tivolis Koncertsal ⓐ Tietensgade. ❶ 33 15 10 12; Ⓦ www.tivoli.dk
Radiohusets Koncertsal the home of the Danish National Symphony Orchestra gives live performances every Thursday. ⓐ Julius Thomsens Gade 1. ❶ 35 20 62 62.

Holmens Kirke Regular concerts and special performances at Easter and Christmas (see page 96).

Den Anden Opera 'The Other Opera' performs experimental opera, dance, performance and other media. ❷ kronprinsensgade7. ❶ 33 32 38 30. ⓦ www.denandenopera.dk

Det Kongelige Teater (see page 63).

DANCE

Copenhagen has a lively modern dance scene, with performances in several venues by 10 or more small companies. Look out for work by:

Åben Dans Production very contemporary stuff often using improvised movement to live concert performances. ❶ 35 82 06 10. ⓦ www.aabendans.dk

Living Creatures Led by Camilla Stage. ❶ 35 81 77 76. ⓦ www.livingcreatures.dk

Peter Schaufuss Ballet Very influential in European modern dance, the eponymous choreographer has worked all over the world and received many awards.❶ 97 40 51 22. ⓦ www.schaufuss.com

Venues for modern dance include:

Tivoli (see page 76).

Kanonhallen ❷ Østerfælled Torv 37, Østerbro. ❶ 35 43 20 21. ⓦ www.kanonhallen.net

Dansescenen ❷ Østerfælled Torv 34. ❶ 35 43 83 00. ⓦ www.dansescenen.dk

CINEMA

Copenhagen has the whole gamut of cinema opportunities from multiplex to art house. Film is usually shown in the language of origin, subtitled in Danish. What you will notice, though, is that some films you have almost forgotten are making their first appearance in Danish cinemas when you visit, sometimes a year or more after their release in other parts of the world. Also you can take alcohol in with you along with your popcorn and ice cream.

Multiplexes
Cinemaxx ⊜ Fisketorvet Shopping Centre, Kalvebod Brygge.
☏ 70 10 12 02. ⓦ www.cinemaxx.dk
Palads ⊜ Axeltorv 9. ☏ 70 13 12 11. ⓦ www.biobooking.dk
Park Bio ⊜ Østerbrogade 79. ☏ 35 38 33 62. ⓦ www.parkbio-kbh.dk

Art House
Empire Bio ⊜ Guldbergsgade 29F. ☏ 35 36 00 36.
ⓦ www.empirebio.dk
Gloria ⊜ Rådhuspladsen 59. ☏ 33 12 42 92. ⓦ www.gloria.dk

THEATRE
Most theatre in Denmark is performed in Danish, so the options for non-Danish speaking visitors are limited, but you could look out for performances by:
London Toast Theatre ☏ 33 22 86 86. ⓦ www.londontoast.dk
That Theatre Co ☏ 33 13 50 42. ⓦ www.that-theatre.com

LISTINGS
The English language weekly *Copenhagen Post* has information about performances and events in the city. *Copenhagen This Week* is a monthly publication, free around the city and contains lots of events listings.

◔ *Vega is a Copenhagen institution*

TICKETS

You can buy tickets for some of Copenhagen's arts events online at Ⓦ www.e-billet.dk

Another option, which also includes sporting events, is **Billetnet** ❶ 38 48 11 22. Ⓦ www.billetnet.dk

Tivoli Billetcenter at the entrance to Tivoli Gardens also sells tickets for other events in the city, not just those in Tivoli. At noon each day Tivoli sells remaining tickets for many of that day's performances across the city at half price.

ⓐ Vesterbrogade 3. ❶ 33 15 10 12. Open 10.00–20.00 Mon–Fri, 11.00–17.00 Sat, Sun.

Sport & relaxation

Sport in Denmark is available to all and facilities range from costly to inexpensive without any loss in quality. Football is popular and there are two teams to watch in beautiful stadia as well as endless playing fields and friendly Danes who would love you to join in. Handball is another popular spectator and participation sport. Swimming pools and fitness centres abound, golf is positively egalitarian, and there's skating, riding, tennis and lots more.

SPECTATOR SPORTS

Football

Played from late July to November and from March to early June.

FC København Tickets cost 120–150kr, more for international games played at the stadium. ❸ Parken, Øster Allé 50, Østerbro. ❶ 35 43 74 00. ❿ www.fck.dk

Brøndby IF Tickets 100–120kr. ❸ Brøndby Stadion 30, Brøndby ❶ 39 69 23 45. ❿ www.brondby-if.dk

Horse racing

Travbane Trotting races. ❸ Traverbanevej 10, Charlottenlund. ❶ 39 96 02 02. ❿ www.travbanen.dk

Galopbane Flat racing course where the Scandinavian Open and the Danske Derby are held. ❸ Klampenborgvej 40, Klampenborg. ❶ 39 96 02 02. ❿ www.galopbane.dk ❺ Sat, mid-Apr–Dec. ⓝ S-train: Klampenborg.

Ice Hockey

Rungsted Cobras Season runs from November to March. ❸ Stadion Allé 11, Rungsted Kyst. ❶ 45 76 30 31. ❿ www.rik.dk

Handball

Ajax Farun ⓐ Bavnehøj Hallen, Enghavevej 90. ❶ 33 21 49 00.
Ⓦ www.dhf.dk

PARTICIPATION SPORTS
Sports & fitness centres
SATS A chain of fitness centres spread around the city. Rates are
around 150kr per day. Phone for other venues in the same chain.
Vesterbrogade 2E. ❶ 33 32 10 02.

DGI-Byen Renovated and classy sports and fitness centre with lots
of courts for ball games and an enormous pool. ⓐ Tietensgade 63.
❶ 33 29 80 00. Ⓦ www.dgibyen.dk ⓛ Mon–Thur 06.30–20.00, Fri
06.30–18.00, Sat & Sun 09.00–16.00, May–Jun & Sep–Dec; Mon &
Fri 06.30–18.00, Tues & Thur 10.00–18.00, Wed 06.30–20.00, Sat &
Sun 09.00–16.00, Jun–Aug.

Jogging
Most of the parks in the city are popular with joggers as are the
Three Lakes. It is safe to jog alone in the parks, at sensible times and
when other people are around.

Ice skating
Winter is the time for ice skating in Copenhagen, with outdoor rinks
set up around the city in Kongens Nytorv, Tivoli and several other
locations. From October to March, if you must ice skate indoors
there is:
Østerbro Indoor Ice Skating Rink ⓐ P H Lings Allé 6. ❶ 35 42 18 65.
ⓛ Mon, Wed 12.00–15.00, Tues 12.00–15.00, 21.00–23.00, Thur
12.00–16.30, Fri 12.00–15.00, Sat 12.00–15.00, Sun 16.00–18.30.
Admission charge.

Accommodation

The main accommodation areas in Copenhagen are around Central Station, Nyhavn and Nørreport. The number of hotel rooms in Copenhagen has almost doubled since 1999 and hotel rooms are on offer to fit most budgets. Outside the city are camping sites and a few hostels and there is a limited number of B&Bs in the city, organised by a booking service, Dansk Bed & Breakfast. Prices for rooms in B&Bs are between 250 and 350kr per night.

Dansk Bed & Breakfast ❸ Bernstorffsvej 71A. ❶ 39 61 04 05.
Ⓦ www.bbdk.dk

HOTELS

Most hotels have online booking, although there will be no great bargains in booking this way. Turning up in Copenhagen without a reservation can be risky but profitable – in the off-season you can bargain for reduced rates with receptionists, or the booking agency in Copenhagen Right Now (see page 150) can find you a room with perhaps a discount. Well into September, though, rooms are fully booked, especially at weekends; if a conference is in town accommodation can be in very short supply. If you show up in one place and they are fully booked they will ring round for vacancies for

PRICE RATING
Price categories used in this guide are based on the average cost of a double room in the high season:
K Below 400Kr. **KK** 400–800Kr. **KKK** 801–1200Kr.
KKK+ Over 1200Kr.

you. You could also consider staying out of town (see pages 125, 133 and 140).

Copenhagen hotels are rated under an official system of stars, ranging from one star, which would have a wash basin in the room, hot and cold water and central heating, to five stars, which runs to video, minibar, 24-hour reception, restaurant and laundry service.

Rådhuspladsen & the west

Cab Inn City K One of the best deals in the centre of town, at the very bottom of this price range, this spotless place has tiny rooms into which they cram everything you could ask for. Nice lounge area, 24-hour reception, helpful staff. If this place is full try Cab Inn Scandinavia or Cab Inn Copenhagen, both in Frederiksberg, same website. ❸ Mitchellsgade 14. ❶ 33 46 16 16. ⓦ www.cabinn.com

Hotel Selandia K–KK Very central and always booked up because of its good prices, this offers comfortable rooms, not all en suite. For a bit more you get cooking facilities. Free internet use at Absalon nearby. ❸ Helgolandsgade 12. ❶ 33 31 46 10. ⓦ www.hotel-selandia.dk

Absalon Hotel KK Centrally located, comfortable, very busy in summer, buffet breakfast in pleasant breakfast area. Free internet use. ❸ Helgolandsgade 15. ❶ 33 24 22 11. ⓦ www.absalon-hotel.dk

Family Hotel Valberg KK Small family run establishment in the western side of Vesterbro with big rooms, nice views, and a good café, family rooms and a self-catering apartment. ❸ Sønder Boulevard 53. ❶ 33 25 25 19. ⓦ www.valberg.dk

🔺 *Hotel Alexandra, a design-conscious hotel in a design-conscious city*

Hotel Alexandra KKK More than just a place to stay, this design conscious, privately owned hotel has rooms individually furnished, some with the furniture of famous designers. Very central and small. Honesty bar in the sitting room. Lovely breakfasts and friendly staff. 🄰 H. C. Andersens Boulevard 8. 🄣 33 74 44 44. 🅦 www.hotel-alexandra.dk

Radisson SAS Royal Hotel KKK+ Arne Jacobsen designed tower block with lovely views over the city, comfortable rooms lots of extras, bathrooms you could set up home in, and egg chairs. If you have money to burn ask for room 606. 🄰 Hammerichsgade 1. 🄣 33 42 60 00. 🅦 www.radisson.com/copenhagendk_royal

Nyhavn area
Sømandshjemmet Bethel KK A former seaman's hostel on the quiet

side of Nyhavn with TV and phone. In summer a room at the back is less picturesque but quieter. ⓐ Nyhavn 22. ⓘ 33 13 03 70. ⓦ www.hotel-bethel.dk

Hotel Maritime KKK At the lower end of this price range the hotel is set in a quiet street with small but well equipped rooms, pleasant lounge area, and free beverages and phone in the lobby. There is a small charge for internet access. ⓐ Peder Skrams Gade 19. ⓘ 33 13 48 82. ⓦ www.hotel-maritime.dk

Opera Hotel KKK In a quiet street behind Det Kongelige Teater, this small friendly hotel offers a 19th-century clubby atmosphere, free internet connection in lobby, good breakfasts and well equipped if slightly faded rooms. ⓐ Tordenskjoldsgade 15. ⓘ 33 47 83 00. ⓦ www.operahotelcopenhagen.dk

71 Nyhavn KKK+ Beautifully renovated 200-year-old warehouse where no two rooms are identical and structural features such as ancient beams are incorporated into the room design, Suites are luxurious and some have lovely views over the harbour. ⓐ Nyhavn 71. ⓘ 33 43 62 00. ⓦ www.nyhavnhotelcopenhagen.dk

Around the Three Lakes

Hotel Jørgensen K Basic accommodation in spotless rooms with cable TV. Dormitory accommodation and shared bath accommodation is even cheaper. ⓐ Rømersgade 11. ⓘ 33 13 81 86. ⓦ www.hoteljoergensen.dk

Hotel Nora KK Occupying four floors of an apartment block, this is deep in residential Copenhagen. Large, newish rooms, en suite

shower rooms. Internet access, some family rooms. ❷ Nørrebrogade
18B. ❶ 35 37 20 21. Ⓦ www.hotelnora.dk

Hotel Ibsen KKK At the bottom end of this price range, the hotel is
in a nicely converted period building with interesting rooms built
into the original structures. Lounge area has free hot beverages, free
internet. Breakfast can get hectic at weekends, so arrive early.
❷ Vendersgade 23. ❶ 33 13 19 13. Ⓦ www.ibsenshotel.dk

HOSTELS & SLEEP-INNS

Copenhagen has some good hostels, mostly well out of town, one or
two of which have twin rooms with en suite bathrooms and which
can work out much cheaper if you are on a tight budget. A dorm bed
in a hostel costs around 100–120kr. Most of the city centre hostels
are summer only dormitory based places.

City Public Hostel K Dormitory only. Make sure you get a bed in one
of the smaller ones – some are as small as 4 beds. Open 24 hours,
bed linen extra, breakfast extra. Pay in cash on arrival.
❷ Rømersgade11, Vesterbro. ❶ 33 31 20 70.

Sleep-inn K Close to Fælled Parken, this is a huge sports hall divided
for the summer into 4–6-bed cubicles. Clean, good showers.
❷ Belgdamsvej 132. ❶ 35 26 50 59. Ⓦ www.sleep-inn.dk

Sleep-inn Green K Small, ecologically sound hostel open summer
only. In the centre of trendy Nørrebro. ❷ Ravnsborggade 18. ❶ 35 37
77 77. Ⓦ www.sleep-inn-green.dk

▶ *Arne Jacobsen design plus unbeatable views at the Royal*

THE BEST OF COPENHAGEN

The longer you can spend in Copenhagen, the better. Even when you have sampled the full variety of sights, museums, shops and other delights that the city offers, there's still plenty to see and do in the surrounding area of North Zealand, easily accessible by local train and bus. It may be touristy, but a canal cruise is a good way to get an overview of the most picturesque parts of the city. Try: DFDS Canal Tours ❸ Gammel Strand. ❶ 33 42 33 20. Ⓦ www.canaltours.com ⏰ Daily 10.00-17.00, 24 Mar-18 Dec.

For the best attractions for children, see page 146.

TOP 10 ATTRACTIONS
Here are ten sights and experiences you should try not to miss on any trip to Copenhagen.

- **Tivoli Gardens** An evening ending up with the firework display (see page 76).

- **Ny Carlsberg Glypotek** Enjoy a coffee while surrounded by art (see page 86).

- **Christiania** A stroll through a unique social experiment (see page 96)

- **Royal Library Gardens in Slotsholmen** Join all the other sun-worshippers (see page 95).

- **Canal boat cruise** Take a waterborne tour around the city.

- *Smørrebrød* Best enjoyed in a traditional city centre café bar (see page 24).

- **Shopping** in the side streets around Strøget (see page 80).

- **Rosenborg Slot** Admire the crown jewels (see page 106).

- **Vor Frelsers Kirke** For the thrill of the climb and the views from the top (see page 97).

- **Roskilde** A trip to see Denmark's old capital and authentic Viking ships (see page 126).

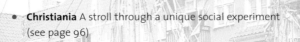

Picturesque Nyhavn is where most visitors begin their sightseeing

Here's a quick guide to seeing the best of Copenhagen, depending on the time you have available.

HALF-DAY: COPENHAGEN IN A HURRY

If you're just passing through or snatching some free time on a business trip and only have a morning or an afternoon – where do you go? Art lovers must seek out the Statens Museum for Kunst (page 110) while pleasure seekers should head straight for the canal tour – sit down and see the lot at the same time, if only from canal level. Anarchists will want to go to Christiania and beer lovers will be torn between the Carlsberg Visitor Centre and a long lunch or dinner at Nørrebro Bryghus (page 114).

1 DAY: TIME TO SEE A LITTLE MORE

Start your day with the Danish breakfast – lots of carbs in the form of Danish pastries, croissants, black bread and mild Danish cheese, fresh fruit and strange cereals, perhaps in the Radisson where you can simultaneously admire some of Denmark's most famous exports – the egg chair, swan chair and coffee pots by Arne Jacobsen. Fill your morning with one of the half-day suggestions, and maybe your afternoon with one of the others.

Alternatively, stroll over to Strøget, shop your way to Kongens Nytorv and then on to Nyhavn, where you can choose one of the Nyhavnside cafés for brunch. In the afternoon head to Nørreport where the afternoon can be whiled away in Rosenberg Slot, admiring the crown jewels, wondering why anyone would want cutlery made of glass and strolling round the park. Your evening should start with a classy meal, perhaps in L'Education Nationale or slightly posher L'Alsace, both serving the best French and Danish combination in the city. Thirty minutes in Museum Erotica after dinner and then head over to Tivoli for a ride or just wander about catching the performances and the sound and light show or (if it's Wednesday or Saturday) the fireworks.

2–3 DAYS: SHORT CITY BREAK

With a couple more days Slotsholmen would take up a morning, doing the tour of the Royal Apartments, admiring the Black Diamond, picnicking perhaps in the Royal Library gardens. The afternoon should be dedicated to some serious culture, perhaps the Statens Museum for Kunst, or the National Museum. Dinner at Salt (see page 74) followed by a performance at the opera house, arriving by water taxi would round out the highbrow evening or you could go on to one of the city's clubs which are just getting started around 01.00. Save your serious shopping for your third morning, checking out some of the trendier shops in Nørrebro but spend the afternoon in Christiania, a place like nowhere else. If you like it stay for the evening – there's usually music of some kind, or just hang out in a bar, otherwise one of the canalside restaurants, say Kanalen (page 103) would make a pleasantly romantic evening, followed by a stroll back to the city centre and a late bar.

LONGER: ENJOYING COPENHAGEN TO THE FULL

On a longer stay you ought to visit some of the smaller art collections, spend an afternoon strolling along the harbour to Amalienborg to see how the royals once lived, then on to the Gefion Fountain and of course the Little Mermaid. A week would allow a day trip to Roskilde and one to Helsingør to see the castle Hamlet never lived in, followed by an afternoon at Louisiana – art in a garden. In the evenings there are movies, the theatre and some good clubs and in between there's always shopping.

Something for nothing

Lots of Copenhagen's museums have days when entrance is free. The following list is not comprehensive and it includes a few places which have not been included elsewhere in the book – the free day or days are indicated.

- **Burmeister & Wain Museum** (page 100) Daily
- **Botanical Gardens** (page 104) Daily
- **Christiansborg Slotkirke** (page 90) Sun 12.00–16.00
- **Vor Frelsers Kirke** (page 97) Daily (admission charge for tower)
- **Statens Museum for Kunst** (page 110) Wed
- **Davids Samling** (page 112) Daily
- **Georg Jensen Antiques** and museum ➋ Amagertorv 4. Daily
- **Ny Carlsberg Glypotek** (page 86) Wed & Sun
- **Københavns Bymuseum** (page 46) Fri
- **Hirschsprungske Samling** (page 111) Daily
- **Nationalmuseet** (page 84) Wed
- **Orlogsmuseet** (page 99) Wed
- **Nikolaj Udstillingsbygning** Exhibition centre ➋ Nikolaj Plads 10. Wed
- **Folktinget** (page 93) Mon–Sat (when sitting)
- **Thorvaldsens Museum** (page 98) Wed

There are lots of other things you can do in Copenhagen which are completely free. All the churches are free, while browsing some of the shops can be almost as good as a museum. There are pleasant walks to be had along the harbour to the Little Mermaid, through the parks and around Christiania. Sadly the best free place in Copenhagen (for some at least), the Carlsberg Visitor Centre, began charging its visitors in June 2005.

If you are lucky you will find some of the city's free bicycles (see page 55) actually on one of the stands and you can cycle around the city for absolutely nothing (but you'll need 20Kr. for the returnable deposit).

Sitting on Hans Christian Andersen's lap in Rådhuspladsen for a photo is silly but everyone does it. Wandering into the lobby of the Radisson for a free seat in an egg chair while you admire the lampshades is worth the risk of being asked to leave.

Another fun free activity is to settle down by a pedestrian crossing (in front of Christiansborg Slotkirke is a good place – you can sit on the steps) and watch people waiting at the pedestrian crossings. Sometimes the road is completely empty and yet they wait for the green man.

🔻 *Visit Thorvaldsens Museum on a Wednesday and get in for nothing*

When it rains

One thing you can do on a rainy day if you don't mind getting wet is to stand in Rådhuspladsen and look up at the Unibank building on the corner of H C Andersen Boulevard and Vesterbrogade. The whole corner of the building is a giant thermometer topped by a pair of moving statues. When it is sunny a girl on a bicycle moves into view while when it is raining her twin has an umbrella.

All the museums, art galleries, churches, department stores and castles will keep you busy for at least a week of rain. Ny Carlsberg Glypotek is particularly pleasant in the rain; you can sit in the conservatory and pretend you are in the tropics. You could spend the whole day in Nationalmuseet and never leave, eating lunch in the café and wandering around the history of the world. Good fun would be to go in without a floor plan and see how long it takes you to find your way out again.

If you have exhausted all other museums listed here there are several more you might want to visit. In Slotsholmen the Dansk Jødik Museum (Museum of Danish Jewish history) is a worthy visit, while the Tøjhusmuseet (Royal Arsenal Museum) is a collection of big and small guns through the ages. In Nyhavn the House of Amber has, besides a large supply of amber jewellery and ornaments for you to buy, a museum of amber with chess sets, boxes and other ornaments as well as lots of prehistoric creepy crawlies transfixed for all time in a shop in Nyhavn. In Vesterbrogade is Københavns Bymuseum (Copenhagen City Museum),with a history of the growth of the city including a quite impressive diorama of the city and, for some reason, a collection of Søren Kierkegaard's possessions.

Dansk Jødik Museum ⓐ Købmagergade 5.
Tøjhusmuseet ⓐ Tøjhusgade 3, Slotsholmen.
House of Amber ⓐ Kongens Nytorv 2.
Københavns Bymuseum ⓐ Vesterbrogade 59.

● *You're in luck – the Unibank girl says it's going to be sunny*

On arrival

TIME DIFFERENCES

Copenhagen's clocks follow Central European Time (CET). During Daylight Saving Time (end Mar–end Oct), the clocks are put ahead 1 hour. In the Danish summer, at 12.00 noon, time at home is as follows:

Australia Eastern Standard Time 20.00, Central Standard Time 19.30, Western Standard Time 18.00
New Zealand 22.00
South Africa 12.00
UK and Republic of Ireland 11.00
USA and Canada Newfoundland Time 07.30, Atlantic Canada Time 07.00, Eastern Time 06.00, Central Time 05.00, Mountain Time 04.00, Pacific Time 03.00, Alaska 02.00.

ARRIVING

By air

Copenhagen's Kastrup airport is 8 km (5 miles) south-east of the city. A very modern and busy airport, this is the principal hub for SAS Scandinavian Airlines. There are 24-hour ATMs and exchange facilities (06.00–22.00) in the Arrivals Hall as well as a 7–11 store, coffee shops, a post office, car rental agencies and restaurants. The information desk is beside the arrivals gate, open 06.00–24.00, and will dispense maps and the useful, free *Copenhagen This Week*, as well as book hotels (06.00–23.00), for which there is a 60kr charge.

The airport is connected by rail to Copenhagen's Central Station. Trains leave every 20 minutes 05.00–24.00 and hourly 0.00–05.00. The 12-minute journey costs 25.50Kr. If you are staying in Nyhavn it is more convenient to change trains at Ørestad, where you can join the metro for Kongens Nytorv. Ticket machines in the Arrivals Hall dispense tickets for both Central Station and metro stops or there is a ticket office. Bus services (250S during the day and 96N at night) also connect Kastrup with Central Station, although they are slower and cost the same. They run every 15 minutes and take about 25 minutes.

An alternative used by some low-cost airlines is Sturup Airport near Malmö in Sweden, just over the Øresund bridge There is a Flybus which connects with Ryanair arrivals, bringing passengers into Copenhagen in 55 minutes. A taxi from the airport takes about 25 minutes and costs around 165–180Kr.

Copenhagen Kastrup Airport Ⓦ www.cph.dk
Malmö Sturup Airport Ⓦ www.sturup.com

IF YOU GET LOST, TRY ...

Excuse me, do you speak English?
Undskyld, taler De engelsk?
Ornskewl, tala dee ehng-ehlsg?

How do I get to ...?
Hvordan kommer jeg til ...?
Vohdan komma yai ti ...?

Can you show me on my map?
Kunne De vise mig det på kortet?
Kooneh Dee veeseh mai di por korrdeht?

By rail or bus

International trains arrive in Copenhagen at Central Station (Hovedbanegården or København H), as do long-distance coaches. The station concourse has cafés, an internet café, foreign exchange, bike hire, left luggage, an information centre (06.30–23.00; ☎ 70 13 14 15; ⓦ www.dsb.dk) and shower facilities.

By sea

If you are arriving in Copenhagen by ferry the arrival point in the city is along the harbour north of Nyhavn (building works on the harbour are under way to bring the docking point closer into Nyhavn). A brief walk or taxi will bring you to Kongens Nytorv, a metro stop and bus hub.

FINDING YOUR FEET

Copenhagen must be the easiest city in Europe to settle into. The public transport is quick and efficient, everyone speaks better English than you do and will gladly offer assistance and although the currency is unfamiliar it is quickly learned. Many shops show the equivalent price in euros, although few accept them.

The most difficult thing for British visitors will be remembering that the traffic is on the other side of the road and that there are cycle tracks along most roads, some of them fairly indistinguishable from pavements. You will notice too that it is not the custom to hold doors open for the person behind you; a couple of doors in the face will soon make that apparent. Street crime, while not unknown, is certainly rarer than in other European cities.

ORIENTATION

Starting from your arrival point at Central Station, the city centre stretches east bounded along its south-east edge by the harbour. To the east across Rådhuspladsen is the long, pedestrianised shopping street called Strøget that travels parallel with the harbour to Kongens Nytorv, a second transport hub, and Nyhavn, where many of the hotels are situated. To the west of Central Station is the other hotel-laden area of Vesterbro.

Travelling north from the Central Station brings you to the Three Lakes and beyond them to the trendy area of Nørrebro, full of shops and cafés.

Between Strøget and the harbour is a small island, Slotsholmen, the financial and political heart of the city and south beyond that again is Christianshavn, with its curious community of Christiania. South again is the island of Amager and the airport.

GETTING AROUND
Public transport

The metro system (☎ 70 15 16 15. ⓦ www.m.dk.) has two lines, still being extended, which connect the east and west of the city with the centre, but not with Central Station. Stations you are most likely to use are Nørreport, Kongens Nytorv and Christianshavn. The metro, like the bus service, is zoned and a basic ticket (17Kr) carries you across two zones and can be transferred to a bus journey within those zones as long as it used within the hour.

The S-train network radiates out from Central Station along 11 routes. Destinations and times are shown in the station concourse and each stop is shown on the platform. You must buy a ticket in the ticket office and clip it yourself on the platform at the start of your journey. Inspectors travel on most trains and often on buses and failure to produce a clipped ticket results in an instant fine.

Buses are boarded at the front where you pay the driver or clip

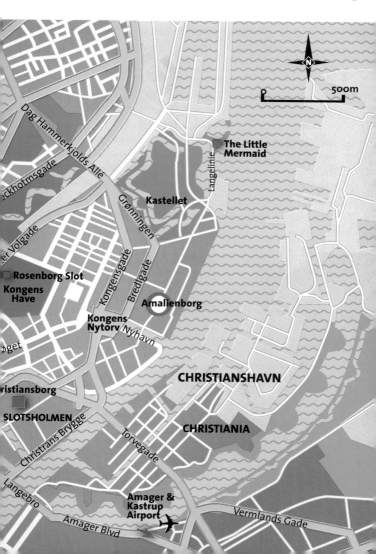

500m

Dag Hammerkjölds Allé

ckholmsgade

er Volgade

Grønningen

Kongensgade

Bredgade

Langelinie

The Little Mermaid

Kastellet

■ **Rosenborg Slot**

Kongens Have

Kongens Nytorv

Amalienborg

Nyhavn

get

CHRISTIANSHAVN

ristiansborg

SLOTSHOLMEN

Christrans Brygge

Torvegade

CHRISTIANIA

Langebro

Amager & Kastrup Airport

Amager Blvd

Vermlands Gade

your bus card. Useful bus routes are: 5A from Rådhuspladsen, past Slotsholmen to Nørrebro; 6 from Frederiksberg in the west of the city to Østerbro in the north east via the southern entrance to Central Station, Slotsholmen and Nyhavn; 8 passes Central Station and goes through Christianshavn; 28 from Frederiksberg passes the city centre (National Museum, Slotsholmen) to Amager.

Single tickets can be bought at the start of each journey in the metro stations or on the bus. *Klippekort*, multi-journey tickets, offer slightly cheaper journeys. You can use the *klippekort* to transfer from the metro to a bus within an hour and within the zones you have paid for. You can buy two-zone and three-zone *klippekort* tickets at railway stations and at vending machines along the bus routes. They must be stamped by you in machines at the metro or on the bus. Other offers include a 24-hour ticket, valid on all transport as

far as Helsingør, and the **Copenhagen Card**, a discount card which gives you unlimited travel for 24 or 72 hours and entrance to a designated group of sights.

Trishaws & cycling

Trishaws, tricycle rickshaws, can be hired around the town and make a nicely green alternative to a conventional taxi. If you prefer to cycle yourslef between the sights, between April and September the city operates a system of free bicycle use. At 125 stands around the city centre are bike racks where a free bike can be removed by inserting a 20Kr. coin. The bikes have solid wheels with adverts on them and no gears. If your trip is in late August do not count on

---

◗ *Try one of Copenhagen's eco-friendly taxis*

The Little Mermaid

Langelinie

Kastellet

Dag Hammerkjolds Alle

19

26

Volgade

26

15,19,29

Grønningen

25

1A,15

Kongensgade

Bredgade

Rosenborg Slot

Kongens Have

Amalienborg

Kongens Nytorv

Nyhavn

CHRISTIANSHAVN

stiansborg

LOTSHOLMEN

Christrans Brygge

CHRISTIANIA

Torvegade

24,19,48

Langebro

5,29

Amager Blvd

5A,47,250S

Amager & Kastrup Airport ✈

Vermlands Gade

500m

— Bus

finding one. Bikes can also be rented from one of the many bike shops around the city for about 70Kr. a day.

Bicycles can be carried on to S-trains and, as you will notice, are easily parked. Some rules of the road should be noted however: bus passengers often alight into the cycle path and cyclists must give way; cyclists may not turn left at major road junctions – they have to dismount and cross at the pedestrian crossing; stay on the right side of the cycle path; cyclists are allowed to overtake one another; when you decide to stop you should raise your right hand to signal to those behind you.

Driving

Getting around the city by car is manageable, although the city centre itself is best done on foot or by bicycle. Cars drive on the right. Car hire is easy and most hire companies do not require an international driving licence. To park in the city you need a ticket, available from roadside machines, which you display inside the windscreen. The city is divided into zones with the more remote areas costing less to park in. Between 18.00 and 08.00 on weekdays, after 14.00 on Saturdays and all day Sundays, parking is free.

CAR HIRE

The following companies have booths at the airport and an office in town:

Avis ❶ 33 73 40 99. Ⓦ www.avis.dk

Budget ❶ 33 55 05 00. Ⓦ www.budget.dk

Europcar ❶ 33 55 99 00. Ⓦ www.europcar.dk

Hertz ❶ 33 17 90 21. Ⓦ www.hertzdk.dk.

❶ *The octagonal Amalienborg Palace is an unmissable landmark*

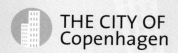

THE CITY OF
Copenhagen

Nyhavn area

This is the epicentre of tourist Copenhagen – the broad pedestrianised shopping street called Strøget is here with Kongens Nytorv (King's Square) at its head and over to the east Nyhavn (New Harbour), the short canal that once brought trading ships right into the heart of the city but now which provides a home for a multitude of open-air restaurants, stylish hotels and swanky yachts. Here too is the Little Mermaid – an overrated but essential stop on your itinerary – and the Palace of Amalienborg, still lived in by the royal family but open to the public, where you can watch the changing of the guard. Further north along the foreshore an old fortress, churches, gardens, museums, the photogenic Gefion Fountain are all strung together along a riverside walk with views over to the new opera house and the western shorelines.

SIGHTS & ATTRACTIONS

Nyhavn

Built in 1671 to bring ships into the centre of the city, the little canal has been gentrified in the last 30 years from a pretty sleazy docks area to a quaint, colourful, villagey little place. The tall multicoloured buildings were once the homes and workplaces of merchants who abandoned the area after a rather unpleasant engagement with the British in 1807 (hoteliers will gladly point out the bullet holes) and for a time in the 19th century three of these buildings (numbers 20, 67 and 18) were home to Hans Christian Andersen, while the street itself became a red-light district. Today Nyhavn buzzes in summer with almost every building a restaurant and the pavement swathed in tables and chairs.

0

500m

The Little Mermaid

Kastellet

Gefion Fountain

Frihedsmuseet

Langelinie

Grønningen

Dag Hammerkjölds Allé

Stockholmsgade

ster Søgade

Rosenborg Slot

Kongens Have

ster Volgade

Kongens-gade

Bredgade

Marmorkirken

Kunstindustrimuseet

Amalienborg

Erotica Museum

Strøget

Kongens Nytorv

Kongelige Teater

Nyhavn

Nyhavn

Charlottenborg

ndebrogade

Christiansborg

SLOTSHOLMEN

Royal Library

Christians Brygge

Torvegade

CHRISTIANSHAVN

Kongens Nytorv

If you want to get your bearings in Copenhagen this is the place to start. Three main streets, Bredgade, Nyhavn and Strøget, radiate out from it and it forms a hub for journeys by metro and bus. The square itself, a huge cobbled canyon of a place with traffic roaring around it, comes alive in winter when an artificial ice rink is set up. Around the square are some elegant buildings – Det Kongelige Teater (the Royal Theatre) was, before the opening of the new opera house, a major cultural centre, staging ballet, opera and dramatic performances in its two auditoria. It will eventually become the city's centre for ballet when a new drama theatre is built. The building is fairly recent, dating from 1872, but a theatre has been on

◗ *All roads lead to busy Kongens Nytorv*

this site since 1748. The statues which grace the exterior are some of the big names associated with the theatre's founding and it's worth wandering between the two buildings through the arch across Tordenskjoldsgade to admire the arch's ceiling frescoes, which seem only to attract pigeons. Carrying on anticlockwise round the square brings you to the Magasin du Nord, once the Hotel de Nord and now a classy department store. Hans Andersen fans can wander up to the third floor, where the room he lived in for a time is open to the public. Further clockwise again brings you to the five-star Hotel d'Angleterre, another grand 18th-century building, where for a mere 150Kr. you can pretend you're a superstar by enjoying the afternoon tea.

Kongelige Teater Ⓦ www.kgl-teater.dk Ⓒ By pre-bookable tour (in English), Sun 11.00, summer only.

Upper Strøget

From Kongens Nytorv the long pedestrianised shopping street of
Strøget begins at Østergade. This street will become familiar as your
time in Copenhagen passes – it's difficult to walk down it without
being drawn into its department stores, or sitting down to people
watch in one of its many pavement cafés. Along here is the
Guinness World of Records Museum, which always has a little
cluster of people around it staring at the representations of people
and things that broke records. There is always something to wonder
at along this street: those people dressed as statues or a string
quartet or someone selling the latest piece of ephemera – Chinese
characters written on to parchment, plastic brooches that flicker
with light as you walk, T-shirts and the rest.

Frederiksstaden

To the north of Nyhavn along the waterfront promenade, Langeline,
lies this royal hub of Copenhagen, a grand building project laid out
by Frederik V in the 18th century in celebration of the 300th
anniversary of the House of Oldenburg. Its wide boulevards and
French-influenced architecture were commissioned by various royal
hangers-on to designs by the architect Nicolai Eigtved. At its centre
is Bredgade, full of classy shops, and the pretty square of Sankt
Annae Plads, whose church, Garnisonskirken, is dull but worthy.

Amalienborg Slot (Amalienborg Palace)

The four palaces which make up Amalienborg, one of which is still
lived in by the Queen of Denmark, were designed by the architect
Nicolai Eigtved as homes for four of the city's wealthiest burghers

---

▶ *The Amalienborg guards even keep a watchful eye on the weather*

but were commandeered by the royals after their own place in Slotsholmen burned down. Architecturally tasteful rather than stunning, the courtyard buzzes with tourists snapping away at the palace guards, who look a little as though they just emerged from a Hans Christian Andersen story, clumping their way around in some Gormenghast-like ritual, slapping their guns and swapping places with each other. A photogenic fountain fronts the courtyard but the real draw is Levetzau Palace, which has been turned into a museum displaying the reconstructed studies and private sitting rooms of assorted royals. What comes over from the glassed-in displays is just how bourgeois a lot they were – a pipe collection in one room, antimaccassars and needlepoint cushions litter another, every surface is covered in family photos in silver frames, gewgaws, trinkets, guns and looming portraits, many of them proving that even royalty didn't always know a good portrait painter from a bad one.
ⓐ Amalienborg Plads ⓣ 33 12 21 88. ⓦ www.rosenborg-slot.dk
ⓛ Daily 10.00–16.00 May–Oct; Tues–Sun 11.00–16.00 Nov–Dec & Apr. Admission charge. ⓝ Bus 1A, 6, 9, 29, 650S. Metro: Kongens Nytorv.

Marmorkirken (Marble Church)

A block west of the palace is this Eigtved-designed whopper of a place, aimed at rivalling St Peter's in Rome, begun in 1749 and due to financial problems completed only in 1894. The church is on an equally grand scale inside, although it is possible to make out the change in marble from expensive Norwegian to cheaper Danish which allowed the completion of the church. The real thrill of a visit to the church is not so much the interior as the trip to the top of the dome (weekends only), which gives amazing views over the city. The journey upwards involves a tour guide, scrambling between the inner and outer roof domes and climbing through a trapdoor, but it is well worth the trip. Take note of the opening times and avoid wedding days, when the church is closed to the public.

ⓐ Frederiksgade 4. ⓣ 33 15 01 44. ⓦ www.marmorkirken.dk ⓛ Mon–Thur 10.00–17.00, Fri–Sun 12.00–17.00. Dome Sat & Sun 13.00 &15.00. Admission charge for dome. ⓝ Bus 1A. Metro: Kongens Nytorv.

Gefion Springvander (Gefion Fountain)

A walk along Langelinie on a sunny day is a treat in itself, with the new opera house on the opposite bank, the tour boats chugging past and, best of all, no pedestrian crossings or cyclists. At its northern end, as a kind of overture to the sight of the diminutive bronze statue that the walk is destined to bring you to, is this much fancier work of public sculpture, the Gefion Fountain. It's actually less than 100 years old, sponsored by Carlsberg and designed by Anders Bundegard. The fountain tells the story of the goddess Gefion, who, offered as much land as she could plough in a night, turned her sons into oxen and created Danish Zealand. It is set in attractive parkland beside St Alban's Church, creates some fascinating effects of light on water and makes you wonder why the little creature further up the road attracts all the attention.

ⓐ Amaliegade. ⓝ Buses 1, 6, 9, 19, 29. S-train: Østerport.

Frihedmuseet (Resistance Museum)

If you are a little perturbed by Copenhageners' sedate, not to say smug, lifestyle; if all that waiting at pedestrian crossings is no longer amusing and is wearing a little thin; then a half-hour or so in this excellent museum will warm you to the Danes again, their tendency to let doors swing back in your face notwithstanding. This purpose-built museum tells the story of the years of German occupation which Denmark suffered during World War II, their belated but increasing resistance to the occupation, the sacrifices of those brave enough to stand against Nazism and their amazing decision in 1943 to ferry their Jewish population away to neutral Sweden in a succession of small boats, in defiance of the Nazi orders for deportation to the death camps. In the grounds, open to the public in the summer months, is an underground shelter used during the war. Particularly poignant are the letters written to their families by resistance members who were executed for their efforts. ⓐ Churchillparken. ⓣ 33 13 77 14. ⓦ www.natmus.dk ⓛ Tues–Sat 10.00–16.00, Sun 10.00–17.30 May–mid-Sept; Tues–Sat 11.00–15.00, Sun 11.00–16.00 mid-Sept–Apr. Admission charge (children free, Wed free). ⓝ Bus 1A. S-train: Østerport.

Den Lille Havfrue (The Little Mermaid)

One of the most frequently mutilated pieces of statuary in northern Europe, this diminutive creature has been beheaded twice, lost and arm once and had several other attacks of vandalism. It was commissioned in 1909 by a beer magnate after watching an opera of the story by Hans Christian Andersen. More interesting is the daily circus around the statue with hordes of tourists climbing out on to the rocks to have their photos taken and the tour boats lined up to pull in close for a better view. You'll still go and see it though – it's one of those things you just have to do.
ⓐ Langelinie. ⓝ Buses 1, 6, 9. S-train: Østerport.

CULTURE

Kunstindustrimuseet (Museum of Decorative & Applied Art)

Housed in what was once the Frederiks Hospital, part of the great

⬥ *The Little Mermaid is usually besieged by her admirers*

18th-century development of Frederiksstaden, this collection, funded by the Carlsberg Foundation, contains over 300,000 items of furniture, ceramics, silver, textiles, carpets and much more. A changing series of exhibitions is produced alongside the permanent collection and it's a little like wandering around a very upmarket, Danish version of Ikea. There is an excellent section of crafts from Asia, lots of Danish design – chairs especially – and the exhibitions are organised into time periods, so that you get a sense of the way design has changed over the centuries. The excellent café is furnished with lovely tables and chairs and the courtyard is an excellent place to rest tired feet after a good wander around. Incidentally in the courtyard there is a plaque commemorating the life of the philosopher Kierkegaard, who died in the hospital in 1855. ⓐ Bredgade 68. ❶ 33 18 56 56. Ⓦ www.kundindusttrimuseet.dk ❶ Tues–Fri 13.00–1600, Sat & Sun 12.00–16.00. Admission charge (children free). Ⓝ Buses 1, 6, 9, 29. S-train: Østerport. Metro: Kongens Nytorv.

Museum of Erotica

Recent years have seen the cleaning up of the sex shops and sleazy atmosphere of Vesterborg, so if you want to study sexually permissive Denmark this might be the obvious place to go. Brightly lit and about as erotic as a dental surgery, this is still a curious half-hour's wander. Starting with ancient sex manuals and working its way through the history of punishments for prostitution, the museum arrives at recent times by way of some accounts of the sexual predilections of a few famous people, pays homage to Marilyn Monroe in the form of one of her dresses and then sets about shocking visitors with lashings of the porn movies that seem to be on every time you turn on the TV in your hotel room. In the warm, almost comfy atmosphere of the museum the videos seem curiously sanitised. There is a sort of shock room – darkly lit and containing photos of physical and sexual peculiarities. This is definitely not an 'oo-er missus' sort of place and quite possibly fails to give any real account of the history of what turns people on, but it is quite entertaining and has a nice set of postcards for sale offering your sexual horoscope.

▶ *The monumental Gefion Fountain is one of the sights along the Langelinie*

Kobmagergade 24. 33 12 03 46. www.museumerotica.dk
Daily. 10.00–23.00 May–Sep, 11.00–20.00 Oct–Apr. Admission
charge. Buses 5A, 6A, 350S. Metro: Nørreport.

RETAIL THERAPY

Here is the heart of shopping paradise, the pedestrianised, café-
lined street Strøget, its satellite streets such as Købmagergade,
Kronprinsensgade – where stores like Stig P and Sabine Poupinel sell
some lovely clothes – and Læderstræde, and the smart stores
around Kongens Nytorv. The two big department stores Illum and
Magasin du Nord are a treat not to be missed, although a good plan
is to start at Kongens Nytorv and just wander. Below are some other
unmissable places.

Holmgaard Dedicated to glassware and crystal. Amagertorv 8.
33 12 44 77. 10.00–18.00 Mon–Thur (till 19.00 Fri, till 17.00 Sat).

Royal Copenhagen Right next door to Holmgaard, this shop is
dedicated to the revered porcelain. Come here to admire but check
out the seconds at Frederiksberg (see page 83). Amagertorv 6.
33 13 71 81. www.royalshopping.com Mon–Fri 10.00–18.00, Sat
10.00–17.00.

Georg Jensen Everything you could ever want in silver. Worth going
in just to admire the stuff. Amagertorv 4. 33 13 71 81.
www.georgjensen.dk Mon–Thur 10.00–18.00 Fri 10.00–19.00,
Sat 10.00–17.00.

Illums Bolighus A department store selling lovely things.

ⓐ Amagertorv 10. ☎ 33 13 71 81. ◷ Mon–Thur 10.00–18.00, Fri 10.00–19.00, Sat 10.00–17.00.

Holly Golightly Big labels with even bigger prices but nice to look at. ⓐ Gammel Mønt 2. ☎ 33 14 19 15. ◷ 11.00–17.00 Mon–Thur, Fri 11.00–18.00, Sat 11.00–16.00.

TAKING A BREAK

The obvious place for a coffee or lunch in the area is Nyhavn, where in summer tables litter the waterside and you are spoiled for choice. Back in Strøget the department stores have cool underground coffee shops or you can sit out on the street and people watch.

Café Oscar K Close to the Kundindustrimuseet, this quiet corner bar serves hot meals all through the day. You're as likely to encounter a shopper as a tourist in here and the menu ranges from huge open sandwiches to kiddie food.
ⓐ Bredgade 58. ◷ Sun–Thur 10.00–23.00, Fri & Sat 10.00–24.00.

Kundindustrimuseet Café K You can admire the Danish design while munching on Danish pastries. Pretty garden to take your coffee out to in summer. Good light lunches too.
ⓐ Bredgade 68. ☎ 33 18 56 86. ◷ Tues–Fri 10.00–15.30, Sat & Sun 12.00–15.30.

Cap Horn KKK Reasonably priced lunches of Danish open sandwiches, herrings, burgers and more. Dinner gets pricey but it's the best of the bunch along this stretch of canal.
ⓐ Nyhavn 21. ☎ 33 12 85 04. ◷ Daily 09.00–23.00.

AFTER DARK

Somehow this area doesn't seem to lend itself to the clubbing late night scene. Most of Strøget's bars are at the western end close to Rådhuspladsen and the Nyhavn café bars seem to close up quite early. There are some exceptional restaurants to try out in the area though.

Fuego KK The best fun around Nyhavn, this South American restaurant flies in Argentinian beef but even vegetarians can have a good time here. Set menus help you though the complexities of some very original cooking. Excellent wine list. Best time to come is on Thursdays' when the meal is supplemented by some Latin American dancing. ⓐ Holbergsgade 14. ① 33 13 11 71. ⓛ Daily 18.00–22.00.

L'Alsace KKK Very traditional French restaurant, with *foie gras* and seafood a speciality. Pretty courtyard outdoor seating in summer and bare walls and silver service inside. Comfortable, small menu, in French and Danish but lots of help on hand. ⓐ Ny Østergade 9. ① 33 14 57 43. ⓦ www.alsace.dk ⓛ Mon–Sat 11.30–24.00.

Salt KKK Hotel restaurant that deserves its high reputation. French–Danish cuisine in an old salt warehouse with a Conran-designed interior. Small menu changes fortnightly but always with a good unusual fish dish. Closes early, with only one sitting, so reservations are recommended. ⓐ Toldbodgade 24. ① 33 74 14 48. ⓦ www.saltrestaurant.dk ⓛ Daily 11.30–22.00.

⟩ *If you can't get a table at Salt there is always the bar*

Rådhuspladsen & the west

Rådhuspladsen, dominated at its south-western corner by the grand Rådhuset, is the place where the city's wheels within wheels are turning. Early in the morning it seems empty and deserted; tables and chairs are drawn up into close huddles, Copenhagen's few homeless people sit law-abidingly on the benches, traffic roars across the huge road junctions that surround it. But later a sunny piazza emerges: fruit stalls, coffee shops, hot dog stands, trinkets laid out on the ground, herds of tourists and shoppers heading for the southern end of Strøget, the long shopping street that leads to Kongens Nytorv. At night the surrounding buildings disappear to be replaced by disembodied blinking neon and the fairy lights of Tivoli. Radiating out from the square is a fascinating series of contrasting tourist attractions – Louis Tussaud's stands opposite the Dansk Design Centre, Tivoli and the Carlsberg Sculpture Centre face off across Tietensgade, the grandiose Palace Hotel is next-door neighbour with Ripley's Believe It Or Not Museum, while lording over it all is Copenhagen's most famous immigrant, Hans Christian Andersen, whose statue sits on the boulevard named after him.

SIGHTS & ATTRACTIONS

Tivoli

It's twee, sentimental and full of utterly tasteless gift items, but does that matter? As darkness falls and the fairy lights hover over our heads, the bandstands fill with music and the rides whirl about we're 10 years old again, just for a while: there are no wars, everybody loves one another, butter doesn't contain cholesterol and the polar ice caps are very well, thank you very much.

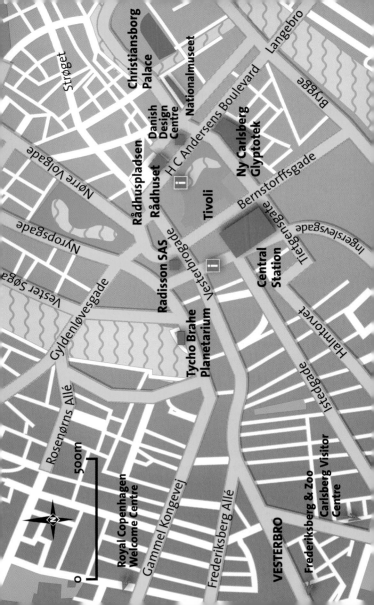

Save Tivoli for a warm night and plan your trip around it to coincide with the nightly performances; programmes are posted up outside. End your night with the sound and light show, 30 minutes before the gardens close. Tivoli has its own fireworks factory and there are displays on Wednesdays and Saturdays at 23.45.

The daytime is for real children, and gardeners. There are over 30 rides (not included in the entrance fee), pantomime performances, funny creatures wandering about, sticky things to eat plus a stall where you can break crockery by throwing tennis balls at it. Gardeners will admire the planting; someone with a real eye for design fills the beds. Beautiful weeping willows, linden and elm trees provide a backdrop to the nightly sound and light show and there isn't a municipal shrub to be seen.

ⓐ Vesterbrogade 3. ❶ 33 15 10 01. Ⓦ www.tivoligardens.com
🕒 Sun–Wed 11.00–23.00, Thur & Sat 11.00–24.00, Fri 11.00–01.00 mid Apr–mid Jun & mid Aug–mid Sept; Mon–Thur & Sun 11.00–24.00, Fri & Sat 11.00–01.00 mid-Jun–mid Aug; Mon–Thur 11.00–22.00, Fri & Sat 11.00–23.00, Sun 11.00–21.00 late Nov– 23 Dec. Closed Oct–late Nov, late Dec–mid-Apr. Admission charge and charges for rides and some shows. Ⓝ Buses 1A, 2A, 5A, 6A.

Rådhuset (City Hall)

Rådhuset was completed in 1905, the work of Danish architect Martin Nyrop. Look closely at the exterior and you will see a multitude of odd figures from gargoyle water spouts to fierce dragons guarding the entrance. You are free to wander about the equally ornate interior but a guided tour would make more sense of what you are seeing. Two things to visit inside Rådhuset are the

---

▶ *Night-time magic at Tivoli*

horological clock just inside the main entrance and the bell tower. This last involves climbing over 300 steps then a scramble further to the spire, where there are some great views towards Kongens Nytorv. The clock, Jens Olsen's World Clock, optimistically has a 570,000-year calendar and its multitude of shivering dials tell stunningly accurate time as well as plotting assorted planetary orbits, lunar and solar eclipses and more. The building has a pretty enclosed garden which is good for a quiet break.

🄰 Rådhuspladsen. 🛈 33 66 25 82. 🅦 www.khbase.kk.dk 🕒 Mon–Fri 07.45–17.00, Sat 09.30–13.00. Guided tours in English Mon–Fri 15.00, Sat 10.00 & 11.00. Tower tour Mon–Fri 10.00 Sat 12.00 & 14.00. Jens Olsen World Clock Mon–Fri 10.00–16.00, Sat 10.00–13.00. Admission charge for clock and tower and tours. 🄰 Buses 2A, 5A, 250S.

Radisson SAS Hotel

Built in 1960, this was designed by Arne Jacobsen and much of his original design has been retained. If you don't stay here you can lounge about the lobby or have a drink in the bar, if only to admire the crazy 60s steel light fittings over the reception desks, swing about in the Jacobsen Egg and Swan chairs or admire the cute ashtrays. One of the rooms (606) has been preserved in its original style and if you are lucky they might let you have a look. In a case by the lifts are some of Jacobsen's designs, many of which you can buy over the road in the Design shop. 🄰 Hammerichsgade 1.

Lower Strøget

Just over the pedestrian crossing begins the series of linked pedestrianised streets, Nygade, Vimmelskafet, Amagertorv and

---

● *The lower end of Strøget offers plenty of free entertainment*

Østergade. The streets here are littered with wares laid out on the ground by some eccentric-looking people, string quartets or drum bands cheerfully busk in shop doorways, little protest groups set up stalls and Scientologists earnestly recruit new members. Among it all at the junction with Nørregade are Gammeltorv and Nytorv (Old Square and New Square), with their centrepieces, respectively the Domhuset (Courthouse) and Caritas Fountain (1608).

Vesterbro

For a long time the part of the city which tourists first encounter – Central Station and many of the city's middle-range hotels are here, as was the red-light district – Vesterbro has become less obtrusive as the big moral cleanup and the increase in hotels around the city has altered the infrastructure of tourism in Copenhagen. There are still sex shops but no more than in any other major metropolis. As Vesterbrogade heads out west towards Frederiksberg the streets take on a decidedly run-down atmosphere, with lots of small ethnic take-aways; Asian and Turkish immigrants have settled in the area. Carry on further and as you grow nearer to Frederiksberg Park you enter the net-curtained leafy suburbs where trendy designer boutiques and cafés replace the fast-food outlets and cheap shops.

Tycho Brahe Planetarium

One for the kiddies, this IMAX theatre uses state-of-the-art technology to display the night skies, as well as showing those movies that make you wish you hadn't had quite so much for breakfast. The planetarium is of course named after the great Danish astronomer Tycho Brahe (1546–1601), who discovered the constellation Cassiopeia (the Big Dipper).
ⓐ Gammel Kongevej 10. ❶ 33 12 12 24. Ⓦ www.tycho.dk ❶ Fri–Tues

10.30–20.30, Wed& Thur 09.45–20.30. Admission charge.
Ⓢ S-train: Vesterport.

Carlsberg Brewery Visitor Centre

Your visit includes two glasses of Carlsberg, so think of the long
walk there as an investment. The Visitor Centre, in a brewing house
built at the turn of the 20th century, offers a self-guided tour round
the history of brewing followed by a history of the Carlsberg
Brewery, which you can smell but not see.

Ⓐ Gammle Carlsberg Vej 11. Ⓣ 33 27 13 14.; Ⓦ www.carlsberg.com
Ⓛ Tues–Sun 10.00–16.00. Admission charge. Ⓢ S-train: Enghave.

Royal Copenhagen Welcome Centre

The factory itself, which was established at Frederiksberg in 1884
and which covered an immense area, has been closed but the Visitor
Centre has a video about how the porcelain is produced and has
some beautiful pieces on show, while the factory shop sells seconds
at almost reasonable prices.

Ⓐ Smallegade 45. Ⓣ 38 14 92 97. Ⓦ www.royalcopenhagen.com
Ⓛ Mon–Fri 09.00–15.00. Admission charge. Shop 09.30–17.30.
Ⓜ Metro: Frederiksberg.

Frederiksberg Have, Frederiksberg Slot (Frederiksberg Park and Castle)

You could spend an afternoon out here visiting the sights and the
park makes a lovely break in between visits. On the south side of the
park you will find a museum of modern glass, the Cisterne. You'll
spot it from the I M Pei-designed glass pyramids that sit out on the
grass. Inside, in what was once an underground water tank, is a
collection of modern and traditional stained glass and glass
sculptures. In the south-east corner of Frederiksberg Have is the

Royal Danish Horticulture Garden, used in summer for outdoor concerts, while the Spa Room holds regular exhibitions and concerts. Beside the Horticulture Garden is Frederiksberg Slot, not open to the public, another summer palace, now given over to the Danish Military Academy and well worth an admiring glance for its 18th-century Italianate style.

ⓐ Cisterne Museet for Moderne Glaskunst Sondermarken. ❶ 33 21 93 10. ⓦ www.cisterne.dk ⓛ Thur & Fri 14.00–18.00, Sat &Sun 11.00–17.00. Admission charge. ⓜ Bus 18, 26. Metro: Frederiksberg.

Zoologisk Have (Zoological Gardens)

Founded in 1859, this is one of Europe's oldest zoos, and although small by the standards of others, provides comfortable accommodation for its captive animals. There is a children's section containing native farm animals, sections containing some of the fauna of the South American pampas, the African savannah and a new enclosure designed by Norman Foster for the zoo's three new elephants, a gift from the King of Thailand. In the zoo is the 40 m (130 ft) high tower built in 1905 which you can climb, if you don't mind the queues at weekends, for views across the city.

ⓐ Roskildevej 32. ❶ 70 20 02 80. ⓦ www.zoo.dk ⓛ Daily 09.00–18.00 Jun–Aug, 09.00–17.00 Apr–May & Sep–Oct, 09.00–16.00 Nov–Mar. Admission charge. ⓜ Bus 6A, 4A, 2B.

CULTURE

Nationalmuseet (National Museum)

Fortunately for the culture-addicted, the Nationalmuseet offers a free day's entrance on Wednesdays. Seeing everything in this museum in one day would be exhausting. A word of warning before you begin: get a plan of the exhibitions before you set out, or bring a lot of breadcrumbs.

The Danish early history section contains a wealth of material discovered in Denmark's many bogs and fields. It begins with a beautifully lit case containing Viking helmets and great curly luren (Bronze Age musical instruments). You travel through the remains of Ice Age deer hunters through hoards of jewellery and weapons, a 1st-century chariot from Jutland and excavated graves showing the personal possessions of Bronze Age people. In room 9 the Trundholm Sun Chariot is a wonder – a bronze model of the chariot of the sun god pulling the sun across the sky.

The upper floors continue the history of Denmark into medieval and Renaissance times with the largely ecclesiastical and royal exhibits, glistering with gold and jewels. The 19th century is less well represented and reminds you a lot of all the other recreated royal rooms on exhibit around the city.

The museum's claim to represent world history comes in the ethnographic section, which is strongest on the Inuit culture, with sculptures, clothing, amulets and reams of whalebone, kayaks, harpoons and other items. Other sections of the museum are dedicated to classical antiquities, including an exceptional collection of black and red figure Greek pottery. A children's museum packs all of this into a few items. Here you can play in the shop from Pakistan, pretend to sail in a Viking ship, fire crossbows and sit inside a Tuareg tent. A section dedicated to coins and an annexe called the Victorian Home (visit by guided tour only) plus a windmill from Christianshavn make up the rest of the collection.

🅐 Ny Vestergade 10. ☎ 33 13 44 11. 🅦 www.natmus.dk 🕒 Tues–Sun 10.00–17.00. Admission charge (free Wed). 🚍 Buses 1A, 2A, 5A 650S.

Ny Carlsberg Glyptotek (Carlsberg Sculpture Centre)

If you are serious about visiting this astonishing art collection, donated to the country by beer baron Carl Jacobsen, you need to plan for two trips (it's free on Wed) or dedicate a whole day to the experience, although you can do it at a run in about two hours. Otherwise you should decide if the French collection or the Mediterranean antiquities interest you most and focus on your art of choice. The museum was built in 1897 around the beautiful Winter Garden, a huge conservatory filled with enormous tropical plants and pieces of statuary.

The earlier collection donated by Jacobsen consists of hundreds of ancient artefacts which the museum uses to trace the history of sculpture from ancient Sumerian, through Egyptian, Phoenician and Greek, including a huge collection of Etruscan and ancient Greek items. The recently opened (1996) French wing has as its basis a collection of paintings by Paul Gauguin, who lived in Copenhagen for a few years, donated to the city by Jacobsen's son Helge. To this collection has been added works by Corot, Renoir, Monet, Pisarro, Cézanne, Toulouse-Lautrec and Van Gogh. Danish art is well represented here too. The Winter Garden has an excellent café where you can eat your Danish among the palm trees to the sound of the Water Mother with Children fountain. The museum is currently undergoing renovation but most rooms are still open to the public.
🅐 Tietensgade 25. 🕿 33 41 81 41. 🅦 www.glyptotek.dk 🕒 Tues–Sun 10.00–16.00. Admission charge (free Wed & Sun). 🅥 Buses 2A, 5A, 6A, 250S.

Dansk Design Center

This purpose-built showcase of Danish design holds largely a changing set of exhibits connected with good design ideas, although the basement has a permanent collection of iconic items –

wonderbras, tetrapaks, Jacobsen coffee pots, Dyson vacuum cleaners and the like. The exhibitions are well worth a look (although some of the stuff, like the rollable home that was on display in summer 2005, is completely off the wall) but there is an excellent shop selling collapsible travel gear and the café is pretty good too.
ⓐ H. C. Andersens Boulevard 27, ❶ 33 69 33 69. ⓦ www.ddc.dk
🕓 Mon, Tues, Thur & Fri 10.00–17.00, Wed 10.00–21.00, Sat & Sun 11.00–16.00. Admission charge. ⓝ Buses 2A, 5A, 6A, 250S.

Bakkehus Museum

One of Copenhagen's literary couples lived in this house, the oldest one in Frederiksberg, dating back to the 17th century and now converted into a museum which honours the Golden age of Copenhagen's cultural life (1780–1830). The Rahbeks hosted a literary salon here and among their visitors was Hans Christian Andersen. The house is pretty much as they left it – diaries open on the desk, replicas of trays of cakes served to the literati who visited here. It's worth popping in if you are visiting the Carlsberg Visitor Centre if only to sit for a while in the small but perfectly formed garden and admire the planting.
ⓐ Rahbeks Allé 23. ❶ 33 31 43 62. ⓦ www.bakkehusmuseet.dk
🕓 Wed, Thur, Sat, Sun 11.00–15.00. Admission charge.
ⓝ Bus 6A. S-train: Valby.

RETAIL THERAPY

Sweater Market Not the height of fashion but they couldn't be from anywhere else. Blue and white snowflake patterns and some lurid multicolour styles. ⓐ Frederiksbergade 15. ❶ 33 15 27 73.
ⓦ www.sweatermarket.dk 🕓 Mon–Thur 10.00–18.00, Fri 10.00–19.00, Sat 10.00–17.00.

Designer Zoo This place comes highly recommended and it's worth the trek out of the centre to find it. Several glass designers working on the premises make the stuff as you watch. They sell their own works and other pieces. Very classy. ⓐ Vesterbrogade 137. ⓣ 33 24 94 93. ⓦ www.dzoo.dk ⓛ Mon–Thur 10.00–17.30 Fri 10.00–19.00, Sat 10.00–15.00.

POD Clever home accessories to take home and amuse your friends or fill stockings. ⓐ Sankt Peders Stræde 22. ⓣ 33 16 17 66. ⓦ www.pod.dk ⓛ Mon–Fri 11.00–18.00.

TAKING A BREAK

Husmann's Vinstue K For a genuine Danish lunch you can't do better than this 19th-century café bar serving smørrebrød. A small menu and daily specials. Nothing fancy about this place: sit down, order your sandwich and enjoy. ⓐ Lars Bjørnsstræde 2. ⓣ 33 11 58 86. ⓛ Daily 11.30–24.00.

Café Nytorv K–KK One of Copenhagen's oldest restaurants, this is far more than a café. Order one or two open sandwiches from the extensive menu of smørrebrød for a big lunch. Herrings are also served if you want to try your luck. ⓐ Nytorv 15. ⓣ 33 11 77 06. ⓛ Mon–Sat 11.30–24.00.

AFTER DARK

Restaurants
Rizraz K Vegetarian all-day buffet with a Mediterranean twist, but also lots for carnivores in this cavernous place on two storeys (and

outside seating). This has to be the best value in Copenhagen.
ⓐ Kompagnistræde 20. ❶ 33 15 05 75. ⦿ Daily 11.30–24.00.

Apropos K–KK During the day a smart café bar serving lunches to
city workers, at night this place has a classier menu, an excellent
wine list and serves modern fusion dishes. A vegetarian menu gives
the place wider appeal. ⓐ Halmtorvet 12. ❶ 33 23 12 21.
ⓦ www.cafeapropos.dk

L'Education Nationale KK This very French Danish restaurant has a
small but tasty menu. The decor could be straight out a Paris
brasserie and the occasional sound of crashing plates in the kitchen
just adds to the Gallic fun. ⓐ Larsbjørnstræde 12. ❶ 33 91 53 60.
⦿ Mon–Sat 12.00–16.00, 18.00–24.00.

Clubs
Cirkus Dinner, show, bar, theatre, concert – all things to all men. New
concept for Copenhagen and so far the jury's still out. ⓐ Axeltorv.
❶ 33 16 37 00. ⓦ www.wallmans.dk

Copenhagen Jazz House Leading jazz club in the city. Live music
three nights a week and Nat Clubben, the nightclub, at weekends.
ⓐ Niels Hemmingsengade 10. ❶ 33 15 26 00. ⓦ www.jazzhouse.dk
⦿ Sun–Thur 18.00–24.00, Fri & Sat 18.00–05.00. Admission charge.

Mojo Live blues nightly. ⓐ Løngangstræde 21. ❶ 33 11 64 53;
ⓦ www.mojo.dk ⦿ 20.00–05.00. Admission charge.

Pumphuset Live rock nightly. ⓐ Studiestræde 52. ❶ 33 93 14 32.
ⓦ www.pumphuset.dk

Christianshavn & Slotsholmen

The two neighbouring islands of Slotsholmen and Christianshavn couldn't be more different if they planned it. Slotsholmen is the political and financial heartland of the country, where the parliament meets and which was home to the royal family for centuries until the palace burned down and they moved out to Frederiksstaden. Every inch of this tiny island where the city of Copenhagen had its origins is covered with landmark buildings jostling one another for attention. Christianshavn, the area of Christiania especially, are a very different kettle of fish. Christiania has, for many years, existed outside of the laws of the city. Its citizens, a motley combination of alternative types and sensible law-abiding citizens, paid no rates or rents and until a few years ago you could buy any kind of cannabis at your leisure in the stalls along what became known as Pusher Street. The rest of the island, Christianshavn, is rapidly becoming a very bijou area with some of the city's most exclusive restaurants having their home in the renovated warehouses along the canalside.

SIGHTS & ATTRACTIONS

Christiansborg Slot

This vast labyrinth of buildings can be quite confusing if you don't know what you are looking for. The Danish tendency to make signs unobtrusive has been taken to a fine art here and it is possible to wander right through the place without noticing any of the doors you need to call in at. A castle of some sort has stood here since 1147 although the present edifice dates back only to the early 20th century. The best approach to the palace is over the Marble Bridge

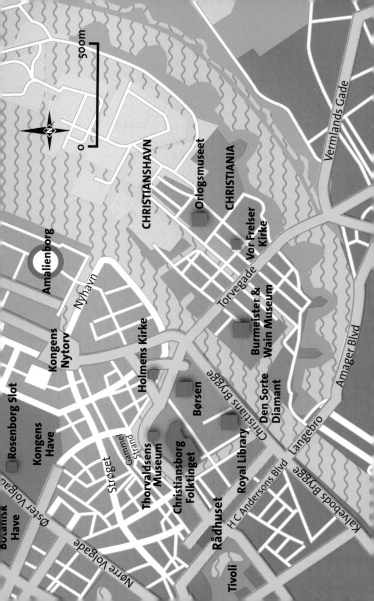

500m

N

CHRISTIANSHAVN

Orlogsmuseet

CHRISTIANIA

Vor Frelser
Kirke

Amalienborg

Vermlands Gade

Nyhavn

Torvegade

Burmeister &
Wain Museum

Kongens
Nytorv

Holmens Kirke

Den Sorte
Diamant

Amager Blvd

Rosenborg Slot

Børsen

Christians Brygge

Langebro

Kongens
Have

Gammel
Strand

Stræget

Thorvaldsens
Museum

Christiansborg
Folktinget

Royal Library

HC Andersons Blvd

Kalvebods Brygge

Botanisk
Have

Østre Voldgade

Nørre Voldgade

Rådhuset

Tivoli

across Frederiksholm Canal and into the outer courtyard of the palace. Over to your left across a parade ground an unadorned and bolted door is the entrance to the Royal Reception Rooms, the only bit of the royal family's part of the palace that you can visit. The visit is by tour only and since the Queen actually still uses the place you are politely requested to mind your Ps and Qs while you go round. Cloth slippers cover your feet to save Her Majesty constantly wiping scuff marks off her parquet, which really is a nice piece of workmanship. Grandiose halls are lined with elaborate inlaid marble, beautiful handpainted wood panelling and a series of brilliantly coloured tapestries by Bjørn Norgaard telling the story of Denmark, including for some reason Hitler, Bob Dylan and the Beatles. Also in here is the fascinating portrait of the royal family which includes several heads of European states and which you will see reproduced in several other of the royal palaces.

ⓐ Slotsholmen. ❶ 33 92 64 94 Ⓦ www.ses.dk ❺ Guided tours in English Tues–Sun 11.00, 13.00 & 15.00 May–Sep; Tues, Thur & Sun 15.00 Oct–Apr. Admission charge. Ⓝ Bus 1A, 2A, 48, 650S.

De Kongelige Stalde & Kareter (Royal Stables and Coaches)

The outer courtyard of the palace is still used as a working training ground and exercise yard for the royal horses, used on state occasions for the royal carriages. The stables themselves survived the fire in 1794 and once housed 200 animals. In those days even royal horses lived lavish lifestyles, as can be seen from the marble columns and vaulted ceilings. Housed here are also the royal carriages and an ancient Bentley.

ⓐ Christiansborg Ridebane. ❶ 33 40 10 10. Ⓦ www.kongehuset.dk ❺ Fri–Sun 14.00–16.00 May–Sep; Sat & Sun 14.00–16.00 Oct–Apr. Admission charge. Ⓝ Bus 1A, 2A, 48, 650S.

Ruinerne Under Christiansborg (Christiansborg Ruins)

Hidden away inside the arch which joins the royal and governmental sections of Christiansborg Palace are the excavated foundations of several earlier buildings. The most clearly defined of them is the castle built by Bishop Absalon in 1167, the city's original fortress, the place which turned it from a fishing village to a capital city.

In a clearly different style are the remains of the Blå Tårn (Blue Tower), Denmark's one-time major prison, where among many others Princess Eleonore Christine, daughter of Christian IV, was held for allegedly being involved in a plot against her father. The ruins are laid out in the centre of a circular walkway with spotlights highlighting identifiable parts of the older buildings. Rooms off the central area display artefacts discovered during the excavations. Captions are in English and work well to clarify what you are actually looking at; the dim light and sounds of dripping water add an air of mystery.

❸ Christiansborg Slot. ☎ 33 92 64 92. ⓦ www.ses.dk ⏰ Daily 10.00–16.00 May–Sep; Tues–Sun 10.00–16.00 Oct–Apr. Admission charge. Ⓝ Bus 1A, 2A, 48, 650S.

Folktinget (Danish Parliament)

Out from the arch between the two wings of the palace brings you into Christiansborg Slotsplads – the main square in front of the parliament building housing the grandiose equestrian statue of Frederik VII, around whose base most Danish political protests are held. To the south and round the side of the parliament building brings you to the unmarked door which is the public entrance to the Folktinget. You can wander up to the public gallery while the 179 members are sitting or you can take the tour in English which

besides visiting the public gallery also brings you to the enormous Vandrehal (Hall of Wanderers), where they keep the Constitution, signed in 1849, as well as some other historical artefacts.
🅐 Rigsdagsgården. ☎ 33 37 55 00. 🌐 www.folkting.dk 🕐 During parliamentary session. Tours Sun 14.00 (daily 3 Jul–24 Sept).
🚌 Bus 1A, 2A, 48, 650S.

Christiansborg Slotskirke (Palace Chapel)
Copenhagen has a history of fires and this church, built in 1826, is no exception. It survived the fire in 1884 that destroyed the palace and endured for a century or more until its renovation in the early 1990s, when a firework set the scaffolding alight and destroyed the roof. All together again now, it is a testament to the genius of C F Hansen, its architect. Its neoclassical marble interior and beautiful ceiling friezes by Thorvaldsen and reliefs by Karen Blixen are a treat and it's a quiet place to retreat from the traffic whirling around Slotsplads. Services are no longer held here.
🅐 Christiansborg Slotsplads. ☎ 33 92 64 51. 🌐 www.ses.dk 🕐 Sun 12.00–16.00 Aug–Jun; daily 12.00–16.00 Jul. 🚌 Buses 1A, 2A, 48, 650S.

Gammel Strand
Not actually in Slotsholmen but a sprint across the bridge by the Slotskirke brings you to a laid-back, traffic-free street for a coffee and Danish while you rest from sightseeing. The strand has an ancient history: in medieval times fishermen landed their catch here and fresh fish was sold along this road by fishwives, one of whom is commemorated in the statue by the bridge; lots of the cafés here still base their cuisine on fish. Also here at number 48 is Kunstforegningen, an exhibition space for good photography.

Bibliotekshavn (Royal Library Gardens)

This tranquil little garden is hidden down an alley off Rigsdagsgården. Almost perfect in design, it has a central pond and fountain and some very complacent ducks, pretty lawns which just beg you to take off some clothes and lounge, and beautiful flower borders. Even Kierkegaard, usually a solemn figure, looks pleased to be here.

ⓐ Rigsdagsgården. ⓛ Daily 06.00–22.00. Ⓝ Bus 1A, 2A, 48, 650S.

Den Sorte Diamant (The Black Diamond)

Beside the library gardens the red brick and Boston ivy homeliness of the 17th-century Royal Library gives way, as you head southwards, to the startling modernity of the Black Diamond, the 1999 black granite and glass extension. Up close there is a definite sense of vertigo as the building sheers off towards the water's edge, reflections of the surrounding buildings on the smooth black surface adding to the sense of confusion. Inside, across sandstone floors, the escalator brings you to the huge library of books and a walkway connects to the older building across the street. Outside the building, students do what they have always done - lounge about in café deckchairs drinking coffee and soaking up the sun. In the basement is the National Photography Museum, which has a changing series of exhibits.

ⓐ Søren Kierkegaard Plads. ⓣ 33 47 47 47. ⓦ www.kb.dk ⓛ Library open Mon–Fri 10.00–19.00, Sat 10.00–14.00. Ⓝ Bus 8.

Børsen (Stock Exchange)

Europe's oldest stock exchange, this place was built between 1619 and 1640 under the aegis of Christian IV, who had grand plans for Copenhagen as the financial capital of Europe. You can't go inside,

as it's now the Chamber of Commerce, but you can stand outside and marvel at the fantasy architecture. Topped by a 54 m (177 ft) copper spire constructed in the form of four intertwining dragons' tails bearing three golden crowns at their ends (representing the three golden nations of Denmark, Sweden and Norway), the stonework is an even bigger riot of embellishments and excesses.
ⓐ Børsgade. Ⓝ Bus 2A.

Holmens Kirke (Navy Church)
The Church of the Royal Navy stands just across the canal from the Børsen and was originally built in 1562 as a naval forge. Around the time that construction of the Børsen began the building was converted into a church for the navy and the present structure came into being in 1649. The austere Lutheran exterior gives way inside to a highly ornate pulpit and a carved oak altarpiece. Several important figures from Danish naval history are interred in the burial chapel and the present queen took her marriage vows here.
ⓐ Holmens Kanal 9. ⓣ 33 13 61 78. ⓦ www.holmenskirke.dk
ⓛ Mon–Sat 09.00–14.00, Sun 09.00–12.00. Ⓝ Buses 1A, 15, 19, 26, 29.

Pusher Street
Far far away culturally and economically from Slotsholmen, just across the canal in physical terms, is this other world of Christiania. A bit like a punk rock Never-Never Land full of multiply pierced Peter Pans who flew away some time in the 70s and never came home, Christiania is one of Copenhagen's biggest tourist attractions, full of wealthy tourists experiencing the thrill of wandering around this very alternative society. Pusher Street, alas for some, is long gone and quartets of Danish policemen, probably the only ones you will see on your trip to Copenhagen, wander around the place making

sure that the stalls laden with hash don't reappear. The dogs which once protected the stallholders from robbery are still here, occasionally engaging in turf wars that only they understand the rules of, as are the cafés, the beautiful graffiti, and wild pot plants growing unattended by the roadside. There are some excellent craft, clothes and antique shops, a couple of good restaurants, stalls selling bongs and pipes, ethnic clothes, and right at the entrance a good café and information centre, also selling some pretty crafts as well as Free Christiania T-shirts. There are no ATM machines in Christiania and no one accepts cards, so if you are going to buy a T-shirt for your nephew take hard cash. Signs at the entrance to Christiania warn you against taking photographs.

ⓐ Princessgade. ☎ 32 95 65 07. ⓦ www.christiania.org ⌚ Guided tours daily 20 Jun–31 Aug; Sat & Sun only 15.00 Sept–Jun). Information centre: Mon–Thur 12.00–18.00, Fri 12.00–16.00. ⓝ Bus 8. Metro: Christianshavn.

Vor Frelsers Kirke (Church of Our Saviour)

This church of 1696, passed en route to Christiania along Sankt Annaegarde, has a worthy interior with a baroque altar and a huge organ that appears to be resting on the backs of two stucco elephants but the real reason to visit it is the trip up the 400 steps to the top of the spire, the last 150 of them being on the outside of the building. Not a journey for those of a nervous disposition but if you can brace yourself against the vertigo there are some stunning views from the top. King Christian was the first to make the climb, in 1752 when the tower was inaugurated. If you are here when there is a church service it is worth hanging about to hear the organ being played.

ⓐ Sankt Annaegarde 29. ☎ 32 57 29 98. ⓦ www.vorfrelserskirke.dk ⌚ Daily 09.00–17.00. Tower open 11.00–16.30 Apr–Aug; 11.00–15.30

Sept & Mar; closed Oct–Feb. Admission charge for the tower.
⊗ Bus 8. Metro: Christianshavn.

CULTURE

Thorvaldsens Museum
Bertel Thorvaldsen (1768–1844) is one of Denmark's most famous
sons. As a sculptor he made his name in Rome while learning his
craft and was heavily influenced by Greek and Roman statuary. His
return to Copenhagen towards the end of his life brought about an
artistic revival in the city. His output bordered on the manic and this
museum, purpose-built at the expense of the royal family, houses
masses of his work. The ground floor consists largely of

⬤ *Christiania is a great place for connoisseurs of outdoor art*

monumentally huge but very dusty plaster casts which were used in the creation of his great works of statuary, set along long corridors beautifully lit by natural light. The upper storey of the building contains his personal art collection. You may recognise many of the busts that line the corridors – Byron, Walter Scott, Christ and many figures from Greek and Roman mythology are here.

ⓐ Porthusgade 2. ⓣ 33 32 15 32. ⓦ www.thorvaldsonmuseum.dk
ⓛ 10.00–15.00 Tues–Sun. Admission charge (children free, Wed free).
ⓝ Bus 1A, 2A, 48, 650S.

Orlogsmuseet (Royal Danish Naval Museum)

Set in a former naval hospital in Christianshavn, the museum is home to a ship geek's paradise – 300 or more model boats lovingly built from the 16th to the 19th century. Many were working models made by the men who built the real thing, to show to their

sponsors, and range from cutaway models to fully rigged, seagoing but tiny ships. There are also carved wooden figureheads, beautiful brass instruments and a replica submarine to walk into, complete with sound effects. There's also a nice coffee shop.

🅐 Overgaden Oven Vandet 58. 🅣 32 54 63 63.

🅦 www.orlogsmuseet.dk 🅛 Tues–Sun 12.00–16.00. Admission charge. 🅝 Bus 2, 8, 9, 28, 31.

Burmeister & Wain Museum

Founded in 1843, Burmeister & Wain was a shipbuilding company that had large shipyards here and was among the first shipbuilding companies to put diesel engines into their ships. During the German occupation the shipyards were put to use for building engines for German U-boats and the shipyards were levelled by Allied bombing raids in 1943. It's a bit sparse on English captions for the displays but ship aficionados can make a day of it between this place and the naval museum.

🅐 Strandgade 4. 🅣 32 54 02 27. 🅦 www.manbw.dk 🅛 Mon–Fri 10.00–13.00. 🅝 Bus 8. Metro: Christianshavn.

RETAIL THERAPY

Carl Madsens Plads is an open-air market in Christiania where you can buy politically oriented T-shirts, bongs, ethnic woollens, skunk seed, bongs and that kind of stuff.

Christiania Bikes All right, you're not going to get a bike on the plane home easily, especially one of those with the huge cart/buggy/shopping trolley stuck on the front, but it's a good place to check out anyway. The best way of finding it in this place, with its

anarchist attitude to addresses, is to ask at the Infocafé as you enter the settlement. ⓐ Refshalevej 2. ❶ 32 54 87 48.
ⓦ www.christianiabikes.dk ❷ Mon–Fri 09.00–17.00.

Infocafé This scruffy-looking café by the main entrance in Prinsessgade has a pretty gift shop selling Christiania-made handicrafts and T-shirts. ⓐ The Loppe Building. ❷ Fri– Sun 12.00–18.00.

Kvindesmedjen The women's blacksmith shop makes all sorts of handicrafts out of metal. ⓐ Bådsmandsstræde 43. ❶ 32 57 76 58.
ⓦ www.kvindesmedien.dk ❷ Mon–Fri 09.00–17.00, Sat 11.00–15.00.

Grønlands Repræsentation Outside of the settlement, along Strandgade, is this centre for Greenlanders, selling handicrafts, jewellery, knives, seal-hunting gear and things made of the hunted animals. ⓐ Strandgade 91. ❶ 32 83 38 00. ⓦ www.greenland-info.dk
❷ Mon, Wed, Fri 10.00–16.00, Tues 10.00–19.00.

Gammel Strand Flea Market Not strictly in Slotsholmen, this flea market is open from spring to autumn and almost deserves to be called an antiques market, with some nice things to take home.
❷ Fri 09.00–18.00, Sat 09.00–15.00.

TAKING A BREAK

There are several outdoor cafés to hang out in for a break in Christiania, although it is not a particularly restful place, especially when the quartets of sheepish policemen are wandering about. In Slotsholmen the place to relax is Øieblikket in the lobby of the new

● *Kanalen offers high-class cuisine in a romantic setting*

library, or leave the place altogether and pop over to Gammel Strand, where there is a pedestrianised area for people-watching.

Øieblikket K Mediocre coffee but some nice cakes and sandwiches; best of all are the deckchairs outside in summer looking out over the waterfront. In winter sitting behind the big glass windows offer a warmer option. ⓐ Søren Kierkegaards Plads 1. ● Mon–Sat 09.30–18.00.

Thorvaldsens Hus K–KK Just one of the cafés set along the canalside, serving salads, sandwiches, filled things and much weightier dinners in the evening. ⓐ Gammel Strand 34. ⓣ 33 32 04 00.
● Mon–Thur 10.00–24.00, Fri & Sat 10.00– 02.00.

AFTER DARK

Christianshavn has one or two excellent restaurants worth seeking out if you want to splash out on a really nice meal. For late-night larks you will have to find your way to Christiania.

Restaurants

Kanalen KK-KKK This high-class restaurant changes its ambience from lunchtime to dinner. Lunch is almost traditional Danish, with lots of people in suits eating fast and failing to appreciate the pretty canalside setting. At night, lit by candles, it takes on a romantic feel with lots of privacy and an almost French cuisine. ❸ Wilders Plads 2. ❶ 32 95 13 30. Ⓦ www.restaurant-kanalen.dk ❶ Mon–Sat 11.30–24.00.

Noma KKK Style and substance in this converted 18th-century warehouse, where local ingredients and methods of cooking have been used to make a very original menu. Bare walls, Danish furnishings (looking a little bit like 1960s G Plan) and wild plants gathered from the Danish countryside make the very haute cuisine worth savouring. Bring lots of plastic. ❸ Strandgade 93. ❶ 32 96 32 97. Ⓦ www.noma.dk ❶ Mon–Fri 12.00–14.00, 18.00–24.00, Sat 18.00–24.00.

Clubs

Jazzklubben Twice-weekly jazz club in Christiania. ❸ Opera House, ground floor. ❶ 31 57 11 92. ❶ Wed & Fri 21.00–late.

Musikloppen Laid-back club/performance venue in the heart of Christiania. Big names have performed here but on weeknights it gets going all on its own at about 02.00. ❸ The Loppe Building, Christiania. ❶ 32 57 84 33. ❶ Wed & Thur 21.00–02.00, Fri & Sat 22.00–02.00.

Around the Three Lakes

The three constructed lakes of Sortedams Sø, Peblinge Sø and Sankt Jorgens Sø mark the northern boundary of the city centre. To the north of the lakes lie the suburbs of Nørrebro, Denmark's new and upcoming bohemian quarter, and Østerbro, the more bourgeois district, important to visitors for its stadium and park, where there are often concerts in the summer. To the south are several significant sights, among them the Botanical Gardens for plant lovers, Rosenberg Slot for history enthusiasts and Statens Museum for Kunst, the Danish National Gallery, for culture buffs. The lakes themselves, surrounded by some of Copenhagen's most exclusive apartment blocks, are lined by shady jogging tracks and park benches and are busy places during the summer evenings, when Copenhageners wind down from all that waiting at pedestrian crossings.

SIGHTS & ATTRACTIONS

Botanisk Have (Botanical Gardens)

Originally part of the city's defensive ramparts, the moat and walls are now a garden pond and rockery in this 10-hectare (25-acre) park, filled year round with excellent planting, which offers pretty bowers, shaded walks a well laid-out tropical and subtropical glasshouse and orchid house. Also within the grounds are the park's little museum, Botanisk Museum, which has exhibitions of botanical interest. Within the park special displays are arranged, including great logs bearing fungi laid out in autumn and a poisonous plant trail.

ⓐ Gothersgade 128–130. ❶ 35 32 22 40. ⓦ www.botanic-garden.ku.dk and www.botaniskmuseum.dk ⓛ Gardens: daily 08.30–18.00

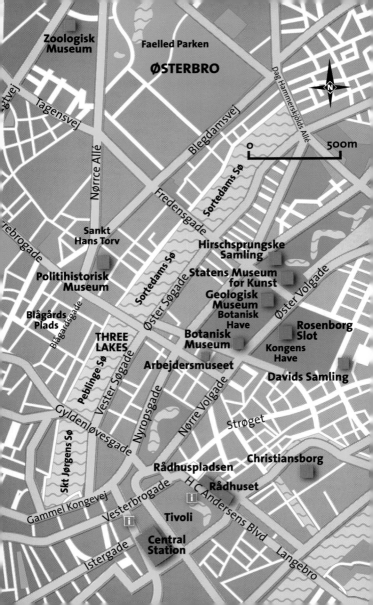

May–Sep; Tues–Sun 0830–1600 Oct–Apr. Museum: daily 1200–1600
Jun–Aug. Admission free. Bus 5A, 6A. Metro & S-train: Nørreport,

Rosenborg Slot (Rosenborg Castle)

You know you're in tourist territory when the coaches outnumber
the regular vehicles, but persevere: this is a lovely little castle, full of
all the things that people who have everything are bought by
people who have more money than sense. The place was built in the
17th century by the fourth of the many King Christians as a summer
palace; from the 18th century, when one of the King Frederiks (they
are an unimaginative lot when it comes to naming royalty) built a
bigger home at Frederiksborg, it was used to store the royal
heirlooms – i.e. all the stuff that seemed a good idea at the time but
that no one had any use for. Here you can see the royal tableware,
including glass knives and forks, a solid silver table, huge silver lions,
endless portraits, all chronologically arranged as you walk around
the palace. In the basement they keep the seriously dazzling crown
jewels and you need to plan your route in and out, since the tour
groups shuffle through almost continuously and you could easily be
trapped down there forever.

ⓐ Voldegade 44. ❶ 33 15 32 86, ⓦ www.rosenbog-slot.dk ❶ Daily
10.00–1600 May, Sept; Daily 10.00–17.00 Jun–Aug; Tues–Sun
11.00–14.00 Nov–Apr. Bus 5A, 6A. Metro & S-train: Nørreport.

Kongens Have (Royal Gardens)

This is Copenhagen's oldest park, created as the private gardens of
Christian IV when he built Rosenborg Slot and laid out in a series of
grids that can still be observed today. It's a lovely space full of huge

▶ *Architecture straight out of Hans Christian Andersen - Rosenborg Slot*

old trees, with a pretty hedged garden and a pond full of very self-satisfied ducks. Kids will love it – there is a good playground and a puppet theatre in summer.

🕐 24 hours. Admission free. Ⓜ Metro & S-train: Nørreport.

.

Geological Museum

Fans of *Miss Smilla's Feeling for Snow* might do well to pop into this otherwise specialist museum. There is a vast collection of meteorites collected from the arctic wastes of Greenland, none of them containing alien creatures but impressive nonetheless. There are also even bigger lumps of amber with their catch of prehistoric creatures inside, dinosaur footprints, a 20-ton meteorite and some remains of 150 million-year-old jellyfish.

ⓐ Øster Voldegade 5. ☎ 35 32 23 45. Ⓦ www.geological-museum.dk
🕐 Tues–Sun 13.00–16.00. Admission charge (free Wed). Ⓜ Metro and S-train: Nørreport.

Politihistorisk Museum (Police Museum)

A little to the north of the middle lake the police museum is housed in Copenhagen's first police station and gives graphic illustrations of what happens to those who cross when the red man is showing. The displays are a little graphic, showing fairly gruesome illustrations of medieval means of correction – perhaps not a place for the kiddies.

ⓐ Faelledvej 20. ☎ 33 36 88 88. 🕐 Tues, Thur, Sun 11.00–16.00. Admission charge. Ⓜ Bus 3A, 5A.

Sankt Hans Torv

The centre of cool Nørrebro, Sankt Hans Torv is a small square which forms the junction of several intersecting streets. It is where all the really tuned-in Copenhageners hang out, including assorted younger royals. In summer afternoons the pavement tables fill with the chattering classes and the evenings are enlivened with clubbers.

Bus 3, 5, 16, 350S.

Blågårdsgade

Slightly more bohemian than Sankt Hans Torv is this pedestrianised street to the north-west of the central lake. It is full of interesting cafés and has a multicultural feel to it that is lacking in other areas of the city. Many of Copenhagen's newer immigrant communities have settled in the area, establishing inexpensive ethnic restaurants and grocery stores. Blågårds Plads, with its many restaurants and cafés, is a pleasant retreat in summer and turns into an ice skating rink in winter.

Bus 5, 16, 350S.

Faelled Parken

To the north-west of trendy Nørrebro is this expansive green area. It has a classy skateboarding park, an open-air pool, lots of children's play areas, imaginative planting and a good café and is home to the huge National Stadium. There are often free concerts here and many impromptu football games. A good place for a break from the city centre, where you can watch ordinary Danes spending their leisure time.

Bus 1, 3, 42, 184, 185, 150S.

Zoologisk Museum (Zoological Museum)

Not to be confused with the actual zoo beside Fredericksberg Slot (see page 84), this is Denmark's first museum collection – stuffed creatures collected since the 17th century and currently housed in a modern building. The various exhibits include Danish wildlife, animals from assorted habitats and occasional skeletons. It has a section specially for children and would make a good rainy day activity. One section is dedicated to animals which have adapted to urban living, while others contain massive walruses, a 14 m (46 ft) long skeleton of a bowhead whale, polar bears and lots of insects. Universitetsparken 15. 35 32 10 01.; www.zoologiskmuseum.dk Tues–Sun 11.00–17.00. Admission charge. Bus 18, 24, 43, 150S.

CULTURE

Statens Museum for Kunst (National Gallery)

In its present site since the end of the 19th–century this was originally the private art collection of the Danish royals, who decided to let the nation share their treasures. The 19th–century building has been enlarged by the stunning modern extension at the back of the building, designed by Danish architect Anna Maria Indrio, which houses temporary exhibitions of statuary. The huge glass north wall of the museum forms a panoramic rural scene in summer which equals many of the paintings inside the gallery. These are seriously worth the effort of wandering through for the permanent collection, which covers seven centuries of painting, and the excellent temporary exhibitions. There is a children's section and there are regular concerts and performances in the new foyer as well as a good café and an excellent bookshop.

Sølvegade 48. 33 74 84 94. www.smk.dk Tues–Sun 10.00–17.00, Wed 10.00–20.00. Closed public holidays. Admission charge (free Wed). Bus 10, 14, 40.

Den Hirschsprungske Samling (Hirschsprung Collection)

Opened in 1911 to house the collection of tobacco manufacturer Heinrich Hirschsprung, this neo-classical building holds Denmark's finest collection of 19th- and early 20th-century Danish art. Housed in a series of small rooms designed to reproduce their original setting in the German-Jewish immigrant's own home, the collection includes works by Danish artist C W Eckberg and his students Christian Købke and William Bende. A booklet accompanies the entrance charge and it is well worth making use of it as you wander through the galleries. Look out in particular for Ekberg's romantic *Woman before a Mirror* set in amusing contrast beside his Portrait of Mrs Schmidt, while in room 19 Nielson's A Blind Girl is a popular favourite.

Set beside the Statens Museum for Kunst, this gallery is often forgotten by visitors in the art overload of its neighbour but it is well worth a visit, perhaps on a different day. Check out the tobacco theme in the lobby with the mosaic floor and the portrait of city's benefactor.

➌ Stockholmsgade 20. ☏ 35 42 03 36. ⓦ www.hirschesprung.dk ⏱ Thur–Mon 11.00–16.00, Wed 11.00–21.00. Admission charge (free Wed). Ⓝ Bus 10, 14, 40, 42, 43, 72E, 150S. Metro & S-train: Nørreport.

Arbejdermuseet (Worker's Museum)

No Danish design items in this engaging little museum dedicated to the working lives of Copenhagen's citizens. Progressing through the various incarnations of Danish home life this encapsulates the hardship of many of the city's working people in a series of recreated rooms, while display cabinets tell the story of the workers' struggle for a decent living wage, sadly only in Danish but the images are graphic enough to tell the story well. Overcrowding and poverty give

⬤ *The Hirschsprung Collection has an intimate, domestic setting*

way gradually to comfort with the few essential items of the 19th century (an overturned table for a bed, primitive contraceptives, cheap, ineffective proprietary medicines) replaced by gramophones, washing machines, table lamps and three-piece suites. Recreated in its entirety is the apartment of the Sørenson family, unaltered from 1915, when it was brand new to 1990, when the daughter finally retired to a nursing home and gave everything to the museum. The café is another traditional Copenhagen construct, selling traditional food and drinks. ⓐ Rømersgade 22. ⓣ 33 93 33 88, ⓦ www.arbejdermuseet.dk ⓛ Daily 10.00–16.00. Admission charge. ⓥ Buses 5, 14, 16, 31, 40, 42. Metro & S-train: Nørreport.

Davids Samling (Davids Collection)
Is there no end to Danish benefactors? This one, a barrister called Christian Ludvig Davids, died in 1960, leaving his collection to the

nation. Besides the Eksbergs and Købkes there is a collection of French and English furniture and porcelain and, best of all, a huge collection of Islamic art, including textiles, weapons, jewellery and religious texts dating back seven centuries. The museum's curators have continued to add to the collection since it became part of the national collection.

🅐 Kronprincessegade 30. Tel:33 73 49 49; 🅦 www.davidmus.dk 🅛 Tues, Thur & Sun 13.00–16.00. Admission free. 🅝 Buses 10, 43. Metro: Nørreport.

RETAIL THERAPY

There is much to see and buy in the area around the three lakes, chiefly to the north where in hip Nørrebro several streets have been pedestrianised and given over to consumption of one kind or another. Pedestrianised Blågårdsgade and Elmegade and the streets which run off from them are full of alternative places, attracted by the lower rents and bohemian atmosphere. There is a big Saturday flea market around the walls of Assistens Kirkegården (the cemetery where both Kierkegaard and Hans Christian Andersen are buried) and another at Israel Plads close to Nørreport Metro station, where on Saturdays besides the junk stalls are some good remaindered clothes straight off the rails of the shops in town. Ravensborggade in Nørrebro is literally lined with antique shops – too many to list here but Montan Antik Design at number 17 and Veirhanen at number 12 are worth searching out. The shops along this road generally open Mon–Fri 10.00–17.30. Vintage clothes are a good buy in this area too; try:

KK Vintage cool retro fashion. 🅐 Blågårdsgade 31C. Tues–Fri 12.00–18.00, Sat 11.00–15.00.

TAKING A BREAK

Pussy Galore's Flying Circus K–KK Set in seriously cool Sankt Hans Torv, Pussy Galore is stylish and cheap, serving excellent brunch and lunch with lots of spiky salads, burgers and more. ⓐ Sankt Hans Torv 30. ⓣ 30 35 24 53. ⓦ www.pussy-galore.dk ⓛ Mon–Fri 08.00–02.00, Sat &Sun 09.00–02.00.

AFTER DARK

Nørrebro Bryghus KK This restaurant and microbrewery is about as Danish as you can get without eating herrings. It offers excellent modern European cuisine and 12 different beers, all brewed on site. Waiters will offer their recommendations to go with your meal or you can try the sampler of four different beers. ⓐ Ryesgade 3. ⓣ 35 30 05 30. ⓛ Mon–Wed & Sun 11.00–22.00, Thur–Sat 12.00–02.00.

Empire Bio cinema Good for some art house cinema. ⓐ Guldbergsgade 29. ⓣ 35 36 00 36. ⓦ www.empirebio.dk

Rust One of the liveliest clubs in town, with a concert hall and a smaller space for clubbing. Voted one of the best clubs by Copenhageners in 2005. You need to be over 21 to get in. ⓐ Guldbergsgade 8. ⓣ 35 24 52 00. ⓛ Wed–Sat 21.00–05.00. Admission charge.

Stengade 30 Alternative music. Tuesday night is open mike night. Check the website for what's on as the mood swings can be big. ⓐ Stengade 18. ⓣ 35 36 09 38. ⓦ www.stengade30.dk

⓿ *Zealand's beaches are only a short trip from the capital*

OUT OF TOWN
trips

The North Zealand Coast

The city of Copenhagen lies on the eastern side of the island of Zealand (Sjaelland) and along its northern shore, served by an efficient, if rather dull scenically speaking, rail service lies the Danish Riviera. To take in all of the sights along the journey, which ends at Helsingør (Elsinore to the English) you'd need a few days but if time is short you can mix and match, picking out the destinations that take your fancy.

Helsingør is the furthest point on this trip at 47 km (29 miles) , about 1 hour 15 minutes by train, Louisiana Museum of Modern Art in Humlebæk 30 km (19 miles), 45 minutes by train, Bakken amusement park is 20 minutes on the same route, and Charlottenlund (for the beaches and the Akvarium) a similar distance, while the Experimentarium is barely out of town at all. The Frilands Museum, a kind of open-air folk museum is a little less easily accessed, needing first a short train journey then a bus but it's a great day out for the kiddies and you might want to check out some of the tour group packages.

SIGHTS & ATTRACTIONS

Experimentarium

More in the north eastern edge of Østerbro than out of town, the Experimentarium is in Hellerup, a quiet commuter suburb where the former Tuborg bottling factory has been turned into a hands-on science centre. A great place for the kids, the centre offers piloted tours around the various sections as the various aspects of science which affect our lives are explained. Very little here involves standing and watching – all the exhibits are designed to get people

involved, from experiencing a gyroscope first hand to making cheese or wandering through a hall of mirrors. The exhibits change regularly but what is constant are the troops of children storming around the place. Bring your own children and enjoy watching them, or come in the afternoon when the school parties thin out a little.

ⓐ Tuborg Havnevej 7. ⓣ 39 27 33 33. ⓦ www.experimentarium.dk. ⓛ Mon, Wed–Fri 09.30–17.00, Tues 09.30–21.00, Sat & Sun 11.00–17.00. Admission charge. ⓝ Bus 1A. S-train: Hellerup.

Charlottenlund beach & Danmarks Akvarium
The Danish Riviera begins at Charlottenlund beach, very popular in summer but more of a scenic green area with a tiny strip of sand and nice views over Copenhagen harbour than a beach, with a picnic area behind it. To one side of the beach is a private bathing area with its own café, toilets and showers and separate nude bathing places for men and women. Close by are the remains of Charlottenlund Fort, now part of a campsite and nice to wander about. The real reason to come to Charlottenlund, though, is to visit the Akvarium. Home to over 300 species of fish and water creatures, the collection includes a shoal of piranhas, crocodiles, sharks and a coelacanth preserved in alcohol. You can watch the feeding times and at weekends and public holidays there are touch pools.

ⓐ Kavalergården 1. ⓣ 39 62 32 83. ⓦ www.akvarium.dk ⓛ Daily 10.00–18.00 mid-Feb–mid-Oct, 10.00–16.00 mid-Oct–mid-Feb. Admission charge. ⓝ S-train: Charlottenlund.

Bakken Amusement Park & Bellevue beach
Founded in 1583, Bakken Amusement Park lays claim to being the oldest one of its kind in the world, although they've done it up a few times since then. It's a kind of downmarket Tivoli, very popular with

Copenhagen families, especially since the 35 rides are bigger and cheaper than Tivoli and admission to the park itself is free. There are beer halls, gaming arcades, a shooting gallery, and at night a popular revue show, together with lots of cafés, restaurants, hot dog stands and other fast food outlets. Next door to the park is another, Jægersborg Dyrehaven, a vast expanse of parkland closed to traffic, with free-roaming deer. Close to the amusement park, too, is Bellevue beach, the classiest beach along this coast according to some, with open green spaces, some good places to eat, clear water which is safe for swimming and lots of brown flesh.

🅐 Dyrehavsbakken, Dyrehavej 62, Klampenborg. 🄣 39 63 73 00. 🅦 www.bakken.dk 🄛 Mon–Fri 14.00–20.00, Sat 13.00–24.00, Sun 12.00–24.00, late Mar–Jun 7 Aug; Mon–Fri 14.00–24.00, Sat 13.00–24.00, Sun 12.00–24.00 July. Admission free (rides charged individually or a day pass can be bought). 🄝 Train to Klampenborg, then 10 min walk to Bakken.

Helsingør & Kronborg Slot (castle)

If you didn't know that Helsingør was a major arrival point for Swedes on a day trip you'd think the locals had a serious drink problem, because a very high proportion of the little shops in town have bottles of booze at knockdown prices stacked up outside . It's actually no cheaper than Copenhagen but it is still cheaper than Sweden. The highlight of the trip to Helsingør is Kronborg castle – where there was never a Prince Hamlet and which was originally not a castle, rather a large toll collection point for ships entering the narrow passage of water, the Øresund. The castle phase of the fortress began in 1574, when Frederick II took a liking to the spot; it was probably stories of this renovation that inspired Shakespeare to set *Hamlet* here. Burned down by accident in 1629, rebuilt and then

🔺 *Kronborg Castle - Elsinore without Hamlet*

ravaged by the Swedes in 1658, the place went downhill for a couple of centuries till restoration began in 1922.

The visit includes a trip to the Danish Maritime Museum, the king's chambers, the chapel and the dungeons and you can pick combinations of two or three of the various exhibitions or pay for all of them. It's a fun day out with the chief draw being the king's quarters, a complete fabrication but with genuine artefacts brought in from other sites. The ship museum is quite interesting, as is the pretty, completely reconstructed, chapel, but the dungeon is a real horror – don't go there if you are at all claustrophobic. The real star of the show is the building itself, set on a promontory of land and looking very much as though Hamlet could pop up on the battlements at the drop of a doublet.

The rest of Helsingør is worth a visit. There are lots of little antique shops, an excellent town museum, with much more interesting exhibits than the great oak and marble things in the castle, and 1.5 km (1 mile) north-west of town is Marienlyst Slot, an 18th-century manor house with exhibits of local paintings and silverware.

Kronborg Slot 📞 49 21 30 78. 🌐 www.kronborgslot.dk 🕐 Daily 10.30–17.00 May–Sep; Tues–Sun 11.00–16.00 Apr & Oct; Tues–Sun 11.00–15.00 Nov–Mar. Admission charge for individual exhibitions.

Helsingør Bymuseum 🅐 Sankt Anna Gade 36. 📞 49 28 18 00. 🌐 www.visithelsingor.dk/museum 🕐 Daily 12.00–16.00. Admission charge.

Marienlyst Slot 🅐 Marienlyst Allé 32. 📞 49 28 18 30. 🌐 www.helsingor.dk/museum 🕐 Daily 12.00–16.00. Admission charge.

CULTURE

Louisiana Museum of Modern Art

The major reason for breaking your journey northwards at Humlebæk is to visit this major modern art museum, founded in 1954 by a private collector, Knud Jensen, in a 19th-century villa set on the shore of the Øresund. The collection was added to with funding from the Carlsberg Foundation and gradually a kind of circular series of single-storey galleries was created, encircling a garden in which are set some amazing statues, many created especially to be displayed here. The nature of the galleries, many of them with huge glass walls, gives the impression that galleries, garden and sea are all part of one strangely lit, complex whole; the weather and, beyond the garden, the sea playing an enormous part in how you experience the exhibits.

The collection includes the work of some very famous artists. Here are Lichtensteins, Warhols and Oldenburgs representing the pop art of the 60s, while Picasso, Francis Bacon, Giacometti and Rothko are also well represented. The gallery also has works by a

group of left-wing abstract artists formed in 1948 known as the CoBrA movement after the first letters of the names of their home cities (Copenhagen, Brussels and Amsterdam). In the garden Henry Moore's *Bronze Woman* sits in her own little area, as do works by Max Ernst, Alexander Calder and Joan Miró, as well as more of Giacometti's pieces. There is an indoor children's area where kids can take part in art workshops and a clever playground in the garden. The café is excellent and the shop covers two floors with lovely things.
ⓐ Gammel Strandvej 1, Humlebæk. ❶ 49 19 07 19.
ⓦ www.louisiana.dk ❶ Daily 10.00–17.00 (open till 22.00 Wed). Admission charge. Ⓝ Trains via Nørreport, signposted from the station.

⬇ *Pop-art heaven at the Louisiana*

RETAIL THERAPY

The museum shops in Kronborg castle and at Louisiana can do serious damage to the wallet if allowed. Louisiana things are very arty, but mostly soft furnishings and some nice clothes as well as art books. The castle is more the cute Viking/Danish dwarf keyring kind of place, with a good line in Christmas decorations at the right season and nice glassware, hand-woven garments and more. For more everyday shopping Helsingør has all the usual stores of a small town plus one or two special places. Along Bjergegade check out Baagø, an enormous delicatessen shop full of open sandwiches, fresh cheeses, fresh olives and more all spilling out of the store on to the street, or Lynhjems Efte Ole Jensen in Stengade, with more cheeses than you thought existed. Further along is Idé Nyt, selling out-of-the-ordinary

clothes, while Crepandia is an interesting toy store in the same street. Vin Og Stoger at number 17 is an antique shop full of curiosities.

TAKING A BREAK

Axeltorv square in Helsingør is a kind of scruffy, downmarket version of some of Copenhagen's squares. Full of shoppers armoured with buggies and plastic shopping bags, it is surrounded by inexpensive cafés, bars that do pub food and some budget restaurants. For a nicer meal you might try:

Solarium Café K–KK in the Louisiana Museum overlooks the sea, with outside tables surrounded by garden statuary. ☏ 49 19 07 19. 🕐 Tues–Thur 10.00–16.30, Wed 10.00–21.30.

Madam Sprunk KK A café bar/restaurant set in a pretty courtyard. Dinner could get into a higher price bracket. ⓐ Stengade 48–50, Helsingør. ☏ 49 20 20 23. 🕐 Daily 12.00–02.00.

If you are out for the day at Bakken there are over 35 cafés and restaurants to choose from and plenty of places for a picnic lunch. Klampenborg, the town where you alight for Bakken, has a couple of places worth checking out:

Peter Liep Hus K–KK It does a reasonable lunch and if you haven't tried Danish food you might like to experience it here. Outdoor tables for sunny days and, important for a place near Bakken, a good children's menu. ⓐ Dyrehaven 8, Klampenborg. ☏ 39 64 07 86. 🕐 Tues–Sun 11.00–21.00.

Restaurant Jacobsen KKK Designed by Arne Jacobsen as part of the Bellavista theatre and housing complex (1934), the restaurant is filled with his designs, including coffee pots, cutlery and chairs of course. One for a special occasion. ⓐ Strandvejen 449, Klampenborg. ❶ 39 63 43 22. Ⓦ www.restaurantjacobsen.dk ❶ Tues–Sat 12.00–24.00.

AFTER DARK

In the evenings Helsingør, especially Axeltorv Square, gives itself up to Swedes on booze cruises as Danish prices are lower and their opening hours (if you can believe it) are more generous. Bakken, too, gets a little rowdy (if anywhere in Denmark could be called that).

ACCOMMODATION

Helsingør has much to recommend it, and if you are really overcome with the scene and want to stay a day or so you might try one of these:

Danhostel Helsingor KK A hostel set in an old manor house 2 km (1½ miles) north-west of Helsingør that has en suite double rooms as well as dorm rooms. Pleasant nearby beach. ⓐ Strandvej 24, Helsingør. ❶ 49 21 16 40. Ⓦ www.helsingorhostel.dk Ⓝ Bus 340.

Skandia KK is a basic hotel with most rooms en suite. ⓐ Bramstræde 1, Helsingør. ❶ 49 21 09 02. Ⓦ www.hotel-skandia.dk

Hotel Hamlet KKK If you can afford it, this has to be the place to stay in Helsingør. It has a good restaurant, nice rooms with lots of facilities and some old world charm. ⓐ Bramstræde 5, Helsingør. ❶ 49 21 05 91. Ⓦ www.hotelhamlet.dk

Roskilde & Hillerød

Hillerød is inland, about 40 minutes by train, a pretty little town dominated by the beautiful fairytale castle of Frederiksborg set beside a lake. Roskilde, 35 km (22 miles) from Copenhagen, 30 minutes by train, is another kettle of herrings altogether; it was once the capital of Denmark and has a deal more bustle about it, with two major attractions for tourists, the Viking Ship Museum and the cathedral, where generations of Danish kings and queen lie not so much interred as resting. Transport to either town couldn't be easier – trains run at frequent intervals from Copenhagen Central Station. For locations, see map on page 117.

SIGHTS & ATTRACTIONS

ROSKILDE
Viking Ship Museum

The first part of the museum you encounter is the workshops, where full-size working versions of Viking ships are made. Next is the museum island, where hardy young men and women are hacking out longboats made from planks or hollowed-out trunks by hand, using the tools originally available. Around them young trees of the species used in the longboats are growing and a few stalls have activities for children. Moored in the water beside the craft workers are some they'd made previously, fitted out for sea. If you are lucky you will see a group of brave souls setting out in one of these boats, which handle a little as if Laurel and Hardy were sailing them but get under way eventually. The museum itself is quite

▶ *Roskilde is dominated by its sober and impressive Cathedral*

126

● Nothing matches the thrill of seeing a real Viking ship

beautiful and displays five Viking ships found in Roskilde harbour, which have been lovingly reconstructed against a huge glass wall looking out over the harbour; with a stretch of the imagination you can see the crews setting out to rape and pillage, their war helmets on their heads. There's also a silly bit where you can put on Viking clothes and stand inside a mocked-up trading ship (they try to play down the rape and pillage angle) or play Viking board games. The museum also has a good shop.

ⓐ Vindeboder 12. ⓣ 46 30 03 00. ⓦ www.vikingeskibsmuseet.dk
ⓛ Daily 10.00–17.00. Admission charge.

Roskilde Domkirke (cathedral)

A wooden church was first built on this site during the 11th century by a man with the curious, yet oddly modern, name of Harold Bluetooth (Harald Blaatand). In 1170 building work began on a cathedral under the orders of Bishop Absalon. The current east section of the church was completed by the mid-13th century while

, the rest is an amalgam of later additions made over the following 800 years.

The cathedral is a world heritage site and its particular interest, other than its architecture, lies in the side chapels built by various monarchs to hold their mortal remains once they had finished with them. On entering the cathedral pick up one of the handouts which list the various side chapels and their occupants. Going round the various chapels gives you a fair idea of the relative importance (or self-importance) of the various kings and queens – some of the sarcophagi are plain, austere boxes while others wouldn't be out of place in Tivoli Gardens. As well as the tombs there are other points of interest in the cathedral, notably a bad statue of Christian IV, the owner of one of the more pompous sarcophagi, by Bertel Thorvaldsen, whose usual skills seem temporarily to have left him. There is an amusing clock which depicts St George slaying the dragon on the hour and a 1554 organ which still works. Upstairs is a museum charting the history of the cathedral, its centrepiece being a replica of a dress worn by Margarethe I (1375–1412).

ⓐ Domkirke Pladsen. ⓣ 46 35 16 24. ⓦ www.roskildedomkirke.dk
ⓛ Mon–Fri 09.00–16.45, Sat 09.00–12.00, Sun 12.30–16.45 Apr–Sep; Tues–Sat 10.00–15.45, Sun 12.30–15.45 Oct–Mar. Admission charge (under-7s free).

Museet for Samtidskunst (Museum of Contemporary Art)

While you're in the town square of Roskilde pop into the Museum of Contemporary Art, housed in the Paloesmålingerne, a former 18th-century palace, where art is seriously contemporary, including video installations and, once a bathroom made of soap.

ⓐ Stændertorvet 3. ⓣ 46 36 88 74. ⓦ www.samtidskunst.dk
ⓛ Tues–Fri 11.00–17.00, Sat & Sun 12.00–16.00. Admission charge.

Roskilde Museum

Near to the Palæsmålingerne and accessible on the same entrance ticket is the main branch of the museum. It charts the history of Roskilde and displays finds from the area from prehistoric times right up to the most recent cultural phenomenon, the Roskilde music festival.

ⓐ Sankt Olsgade 18. ❶ 46 31 65 65. ⓦ www. roskildemuseum.dk. ❶ Daily 11.00–16.00. Admission charge.

HILLERØD
Frederiksborg Slot

We have Frederik II to thank for this dramatic piece of real estate, set on a series of islands in a man-made lake and surrounded by gardens recently restored to their baroque stateliness. Like Rosenborg (see page 106), the site was a summer palace, built in 1560. The next owner of the place, Christian IV, built an even bigger structure in the Dutch Renaissance style to a design by Hans van Steenwinckel.

You enter the palace through an open courtyard dominated by the Neptune Fountain, a 19th-century replica of an original that was destroyed during the Swedish occupation. The main body of the castle, destroyed first by the Swedes and then by fire in 1859, was saved when the Carlsberg Foundation stepped up yet again, and in 1882 began the restoration and conversion to a national museum. And as museums go, it's pretty good – there is a kind of a theme running through the castle's collections. Danish history is seen through the perspective of its royal family, a series of paintings of moments from Denmark's history and portraits of the kings and queens.

The chapel, where Danish kings were crowned for nearly two

centuries, survived fire and the Swedes intact and is a stunningly ornate place, especially when the sun bursts through the stained glass. Above it, the Great Hall didn't do so well in the fire but although it is a reconstruction it is still amazing – stand still and look at the artwork on the ceiling. The third floor serves as a national portrait gallery, with Danish worthies painted by some fairly famous names, including Andy Warhol (he painted the present Queen). As you wander round admiring the artwork, take a look out of the windows along the north-east wall of the house for beautiful views over the baroque garden.

☎ 48 26 04 39. ⓦ www.frederiksborgmuseet.dk ⏰ Daily 10.00–17.00 Apr–Oct, 11.00–15.00 Nov–Mar. Admission charge.

RETAIL THERAPY

In Roskilde shopping has a quietly suburban feel to it. The shopping streets are largely pedestrianised and tables sit out on the pavements with busy shoppers taking a break. That's not to say that there aren't a couple of places worth investigating. At **Strædet 2** the shop of the same name sells some pretty clothes and soft furnishings – a sort of hand-picked Laura Ashley. Along Algade are several interesting shops. At number 10 the department store **Inspiration** deserves a few minutes browsing, while further along the street at number 37 is Butik Jane Onø, one of those shops which doesn't quite know what it sells but it's all nice – coffee beans, crockery, candles, cushions, light fittings, perfume, marmalade, chocolates. Just the smells wafting up from the chocolate and coffee beans are worth a visit. Here too is a branch of **Tiger**, a chain store with outlets all over the place, but this is a particularly good one. All its goods cost either 10Kr. or 20Kr. and lots of them are

useful and attractive: cheap herbs and spices, over-the-counter reading glasses, slippers, candles. There are hours of browsing in these shops. The **Viking Ship Museum** has lots of Viking-related things (but not the helmets, sadly), while in an old gasworks building beside the Viking Ship Museum are two places which are almost sights in their own right. **Glassgalleriet** (❸ Vinboder 1) is a craft shop where the pieces, all glass, are hand-made on the premises. Next door is the Roskildegalleriet, a warren of galleries showing the work of local artists.

In Hillerød close by the castle is a craft shop selling patterned jumpers, pottery and the like. The castle shop is well worth a browse too.

TAKING A BREAK

Roskilde
Next door to Strædet 2 (see under Retail Therapy) is the pleasant **Café Satchmo**, good for a cup of coffee and Danish before setting off for the cathedral. In Skomagergade, the pedestrianised street south of the cathedral, you'll find any number of pleasant places to stop for a break.

HILLERØD
The best place for lunch or just a good coffee in Fredericksborg is **Spisestedet Leonora**, in the castle grounds (🕒 10.00–17.00).

AFTER DARK

Roskilde
There's not much to do in Roskilde unless it's the last weekend in

June, when for four days the population doubles and music fills the streets at the Roskilde Festival.

Restaurant Bryggegården K–KK A café bar which pours out onto the street on sunny days. Big pub food menu on boards outside and a more bar-like atmosphere in the evening. ⓐ Aldgade 15. ⓣ 46 35 01 03. ⓛ Daily 11.00–23.00.

Restaurant Snekken K–KK Close to the Viking Ship Museum and overlooking Roskilde harbour, this place has outdoor tables in summer and serves good Danish–Mediterranean-style food. ⓐ Vindeboder 16. ⓛ Daily 11.30–16.30, 18.30–21.30.

Hillerød
Den Gale Coq This is a good option for an evening meal. ⓐ Helsingørgade 16.

ACCOMMODATION

Roskilde
Roskilde Vandrerhjem K Newish hostel with double rooms, family rooms, all en suite and nice views of the harbour. Throw in cooking facilities and it's worth the stay. ⓐ Vindeboder 7. ⓣ 46 35 21 84; ⓦ www.danhostel.dk/roskilde

Hotel Prinsden KKK Denmark's oldest hotel. Lots of charm and a long list of worthies in its guest book. Algade 13. ⓣ 46 30 91 00. ⓦ www.prinsden.dk

Amager

The route from the airport into town by train seems to be a series of building sites as the countryside to the south and east of Copenhagen is developed. The places of interest to tourists in this area are on the flat, culturally distinct island of Amager, linked to Copenhagen by a series of bridges and now to Malmo in Sweden by both road and rail. A gigantic shopping mall is on its way, the national television centre is due to open there, it is home to the airport and buildings are sprouting by the day. As yet it's still a nice quiet area, with lots of good beaches along the eastern coastline, a big nature reserve on the western side and some pretty villages. Ishoj, 17 km (11 miles) west of the city centre, is a working-class suburb of the city, its chief claim to fame being Arken, the disorientating museum of modern art built right out on the seashore. Both areas are easily accessible by bus and train. For location see map on page 117.

Twenty minutes by bus from the centre of Copenhagen, Amager is still, despite the building programmes and improved transport, an island that can offer some quiet beaches as well as the pretty seaside town of Dragør. It doesn't have the golden beaches and beautiful people of the Danish Riviera; its seascapes are industrial and its beaches a little stony but they can be quite deserted. Its eastern coastline is a string of good beaches with shallow water, good for paddling. On the western side on reclaimed land is Kalvebod Faelled, a huge nature reserve, created during World War II to provide work for Danish men who might otherwise have been transported to Germany to work in the munitions factories. It was

▶ *The startling Ark Museum of Modern Art*

used for many years as a firing range before the wildlife park was created. An interpretive centre for the nature reserve offers bikes for hire and use of a campsite in the reserve. Closer to town is Islands Brygge, a very cool suburb of Copenhagen with a really interesting outdoor swimming pool and some nice walks along the waterfront.
Kalvebod Faelled ❶ 35 52 04 03. Ⓜ Metro: Vestamager.

SIGHTS & ATTRACTIONS

Arken Museum for Moderne Kunst (Ark Museum of Modern Art)
Almost too much to take in, the Ark stands on an inaccessible windswept beach reclaimed from Køge Bay. It opened, to much acclaim, in 1996, Copenhagen's year as European City of Culture, and was originally intended to be built out in the bay itself but the cost and environmental consequences were just too great and to the architect Søren Robert Lund's chagrin it stayed on land. The building is designed to look like a great concrete and steel ship which has beached itself on land and has a startling effect on the shoreline when viewed from a distance. Many critics say that the curiosity value of the building itself detracts from the art on display inside; unlike Louisiana this building doesn't blend art, garden and seascape, it demands attention that should be given over to the exhibitions inside.

The museum has a permanent collection but its chief exhibits are temporary displays, often of very contemporary works; often the cinema is the venue for seeing some of the material. Check the website before trekking out here to see what is on. The restaurant on the first floor has great views over the bay and the toilets are pretty cool too.

The gallery stands on a long reclaimed beach running between the towns of Brøndby and Hundige and makes an excellent place for a quiet afternoon if you want to get away from the city.

ⓐ Skovvej 100, Ishøj. ⓣ 43 54 02 22. ⓦ www.arken.dk
ⓛ Tues, Thur–Sun 10.00–17.00, Wed 10.00–21.00. Admission charge.
ⓝ Train to Ishøj, then Bus 128.

Amager Museum

This folksy kind of place is more than just the local museum filled with bits and pieces turned up in back gardens. It tells the history of the people who settled and farmed here by showing you exactly how they did it. Set in two old Dutch farms (the settlers here came from Holland in the 16th century) the museum grows vegetables in the old style, while its curators, dressed in traditional clothes, take you through the various farm processes from cheese- and butter-making to looking after the animals. The museum is at Store Magleby en route to Dragør by road.

ⓐ Hovedgade 4 & 12, Store Magleby. ⓣ 32 53 02 50.
ⓦ www.dragoerinformation.dk ⓛ Tues–Sun 12.00–16.00
May–Sep(Wed and Sun only Oct–Apr). Admission charge.
ⓝ Bus 30, 73.

Islands Brygge

Walkable from Christianshavn, this suburb of the city is rapidly taking on a very bohemian atmosphere with lots of art galleries opening up in the cheaper and bigger accommodation on offer here. Look up **Galleri Christina Wilson** at Sturlasgade 12H, **GIMM E15** at number 14D, and **I-N-K, Nils Stæk** and **Galleri Nicolai Wallner** at numbers 21H, 19C and 21 respectively. ⓝ Bus 33, 40. Metro: Islands Brygge.

Dragør

If you want to experience at first hand a complete Danish community in all its *hygge* a good place to visit is the tiny cobbled village of Dragør on the east coast of Amager. Picture-postcard perfect, the village seems fixed in a little time capsule where hollyhocks and tiny pruned bay trees are tended in the cracks between houses and cobbles and the heat of the sun glows off the orange tiled roofs. This village has been here since the 14th century, when it prospered as a fishing port. Sinking into a decline when steam and diesel powered ships made the sea trade uneconomical for small fishermen, the village remained untouched for a century or so until the airport, the bridge and, most importantly, the metro made it into a very desirable suburb of the city. The village square is fronted with houses dating back to the late 18th century while the obelisk at its centre marks the distance from Copenhagen – 1¹/₂ Danish miles. Dragør has a tiny museum close to the harbour containing seafaring memorabilia and a history of the village.
ⓐ Havnepladsen Strandlinien 2. ❶ 32 53 41 06; ⓦ www.dragoer-information.dk ◷ Tues–Sun 12.00–16.00 May–Sep. Admission charge. Ⓝ Bus 30, 32, 73.

RETAIL THERAPY

The most fun you can have shopping on the island of Amager is at the weekend indoor flea market in Holmbladsgade, close to the city centre. In the suburbs of Islands Brygge a few unusual shops are worth searching out.

Det Piå Pakhus Copenhagen's largest indoor flea market. Makes Israel Plads (see page 113) look amateurish. Hundreds of stalls of second-hand stuff, bric-a-brac and antiques. ⓐ Holmbladsgade 113, Amager. ⓛ Sat & Sun 10.00–17.00.

X One of those shops that you go in to browse and come out with something you never knew you wanted. Jewellery, locally made crafts and art pieces, homewares, crazy footwear. Take note of the opening hours – these people don't believe in overworking! ⓐ Isafjordsgade 6, Islands Brygge. ⓛ Tues–Fri 15.00–18.00, Sat 10.00–14.00.

TAKING A BREAK & AFTER DARK

There's not much to keep you after dark in Amager although the café in Arken is great for views as well as good lunches and brunches – the room seems to hang out into the sea and is full of light and seascapes. The good places to eat in Dragør wouldn't keep you there for an evening either, unless of course you turn up in the last weekend in July when the village celebrates its annual music festival (ⓦ www.dragoermusikfest.dk). At Amager beach a few

● *Islands Brygge is laid-back, even by Copenhagen standards*

multicoloured beach bars offer sensible drinks and snacks. At Islands Brygge are two cafés that can be highly recommended if you are in the area.

Arken Café K a Skovvej 100, Ishøj. ☎ 43 57 34 21. 🕙 10.00–16.30 Tues–Sun.

Café Alma K–KK A comfortable place to sit and watch the world go by, this place serves good coffee and light meals including a good vegetarian option. a Isafjordsgade 5, Islands Brygge. ☎ 32 54 32 04. 🕙 Mon–Fri 11.00–24.00, Sat & Sun 10.00–24.00.

Café Saga K–KK Recently opened and voted by Copenhageners the best new café of 2005, this place in the bohemian quarter of Islands Brygge, close to Christianshavn, has sunny outdoor seating and some very reasonable prices. a Egilsgade 20, Islands Brygge. ☎ 32 57 17 24. 🌐 www.cafesaga.aok.dk

Beghuset KK This quite reasonably priced place is reputedly the best that Dragør has to offer – comfortable Danish–French cooking and lots of locals having family reunions. a Standgade 14, Dragør. ☎ 32 53 01 36. 🕙 Tues–Sun 12.00–15.00, 18.00–21.30.

ACCOMMODATION

Belægningen K Newish hostel with lots of facilities and some double rooms. Free internet, bike rental. Close to metro. a Avedørelejren, Vester Kvartegade 22, Hvidovre. ☎ 36 77 90 84. 🌐 www.belaegningen.dk

> ● *Not all the police carry light sabres!*

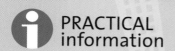

PRACTICAL
information

Directory

GETTING THERE

By air

Ticketless budget airlines are often the cheapest way to travel. They offer off-peak and late or early flights at very low rates, occasionally for little more than the airport charges. You will find prices are lower the earlier you book; a ticket booked the day before you leave will cost much more than one on the same flight booked weeks in advance. Prices also go up at peak times such as the school and public holidays, at weekends and when there is an event on in Copenhagen. All the airlines have websites which will display schedules and prices. Special offers are often advertised in newspapers.

British airports, including London, Birmingham, Manchester, Aberdeen, Glasgow and Edinburgh, have direct flights to Copenhagen, as does Dublin. Flying time from London airports is around 1 hr 45 minutes. Ryanair flies from London Stansted and Luton to Malmö in Sweden, which is only a short road or rail journey from Copenhagen. Airlines offering these flights to Copenhagen include:

Aer Lingus (from Dublin) Ⓦ www.aerlingus.com
British Airways Ⓦ www.ba.com
British Midland Ⓦ www.flybmi.com
Easyjet Ⓦ www.easyjet.com
Maersk Ⓦ www.maersk-air.co.uk
Ryanair (to Malmö) Ⓦ www.ryanair.com
SAS (from UK and Dublin) Ⓦ www.scandinavian.net
Varig Ⓦ www.varig.com

By rail

This is normally the most expensive way to get to Copenhagen, but not if you are visiting the city as part of an Interrail or Eurail trip. Rail Europe can book the journey on line. A direct journey from the UK by rail will involve a cross-Channel ferry or the Eurostar to Brussels as the first leg of your journey. The monthly *Thomas Cook European Rail Timetable* has up-to-date schedules for international train services to Copenhagen and many Danish domestic routes.

Rail Europe www.raileurope.co.uk
Eurostar Reservations (UK) ☎ 08705 186186 🌐 www.eurostar.com
Thomas Cook European Rail Timetable ☎ (UK) 01733 416477; (USA) 1 800 322 3834. 🌐 www.thomascookpublishing.com

By ferry

If you plan to bring your own car to Copenhagen, one way to arrive there is by ferry from Harwich to Esjberg with DFDS Seaways. Departures are all year round, three times a week. If you are approaching Copenhagen via Malmö the car ferry is 35 minutes and from Oslo 16 hours.

DFDS Seaways ☎ 08705 333 000 🌐 www.dfdsseaways.co.uk

ENTRY FORMALITIES
Documentation

EU, US, Canadian, Australian and New Zealand citizens need only to bring a valid passport. Other nationalities may need a visa. For stays longer than 3 months a residence permit is required; EU citizens must apply for one while in Denmark, other nationals must obtain one before arrival. Immigration control is stricter than EU citizens may be used to; immigration officers may ask for proof that you have a means of support for your stay in the country, that you have somewhere to stay and what the purpose of your visit is.

Customs

Residents of the UK, Ireland and other EU countries may bring into Denmark personal possessions and goods for personal use, including a reasonable amount of tobacco and alcohol, provided they have been bought in the EU. There are few formalities at the point of entry into Denmark. Residents of non-EU countries, and EU residents arriving from a non-EU country, may bring in up to 400 cigarettes and 50 cigars or 50g (2 oz) tobacco; 2 litres (3 bottles) of wine and 1 litre (approx. 2 pints) of spirits or liqueurs.

MONEY

Denmark is not part of the eurozone. Its currency, the krone (Kr), is divided into smaller units called øre. Notes come in 50, 100, 200, 500 and 1000Kr. while the coins are 1, 2, 5, 10 and 20Kr and 25 and 50 øre. Banks are plentiful. Their opening hours are 10.00–16.00 weekdays, sometimes till 18.00 on Thursdays. The Den Danske Bank at Central Station is open daily 08.00–20.00 but the commission on exchange is higher after banking hours. 24-hour ATMs are even more plentiful than banks and accept most internationally recognised debit and credit cards. Most banks will exchange a wide range of currencies and you can usually buy items on the plane or ferry in your own currency, although you'll get a terrible exchange rate and change in kroner. Visa and Mastercard are widely accepted in shops and restaurants.

HEALTH, SAFETY & CRIME

No precautions in terms of vaccination or preventive medicines need be taken before visiting Copenhagen. Tap water is safe to drink and health care is excellent. EU citizens are entitled to make use of the Danish health care system although they must show the new European Health Insurance Card (EHIC) and may have to reclaim their expenses once they have returned home. Emergency treatment is free to all visitors and many countries outside the EU have similar reciprocal agreements. Travel insurance is still essential in order to cover the cost of an emergency flight back to your country of origin. A consultation with a doctor as a private patient will cost around 500Kr.

Copenhagen is one of the safest cities in Europe. Visitors should nevertheless always take care of their belongings, especially in crowded places such as the Central Station. Strøget in the early hours may be problematic, as the bars turn out, and in some areas around Vesterbro and Nørrebro you should be cautious. If you have anything stolen, report it immediately to the police and obtain a copy of their report for your insurance claim. A greater danger to visitors may be the system of cycle lanes, which run along most streets in the city, occasionally against the flow of traffic. In some cases the distinction between the cycle lane and the pedestrian area is simply a set of footprints painted on to the pavement to indicate where pedestrians can walk.

OPENING HOURS

On weekdays shops open at around 10.00 and close somewhere between 17.30 and 18.00, although some may stay open later. On Saturdays most shops are closed by mid-afternoon and will remain closed on Sundays, although bakeries open Sunday morning. Office hours are Mon–Fri 09.00–16.00.

TOILETS

There is no shortage of clean, user-friendly public toilets in Copenhagen. The toilets in Central Station have good and inexpensive showers. Most public squares have pleasant public toilets, as do department stores, and if you are desperate there are always bars and cafés.

CHILDREN

Copenhagen is a child-friendly city. Most restaurants and café bars can accommodate them and have child seats and highchairs and some even have child menus. Trains and buses have areas set aside for buggies and buses have easy access. Most museums and art galleries provide special children's sections and there are several sights in the city that will impress your children more than you.

The beaches and parks are a useful resource for those with children, especially in summer when there are often puppet shows in the parks. Out of town the Akvarium (see page 118) and the Experimentarium (page 116) are good for children, with lots of hands-on exhibits, and Louisiana (page 121) has a children's art room where kids can experiment with different media. Bike shops hire out children's bikes as well as adults. Bakken (page 118) and Tivoli (page 76) are also likely to keep your kids entertained.

Nationalmuseet (page 84) has a children's museum which reduces all of history to child-comprehensible packages and has an early school room where they can explore the ink wells. Statens Museum for Kunst (page 110) has a children's section where children can explore their artistic skills and displays some child-suitable material. There are also performances in the lobby which will interest children.

Orlogsmuseet (page 99) has a children's section where they can handle guns and climb around a submarine. The Viking ship Museum in Roskilde (page 126) has mocked-up ships and things to

● *Give the kids a breath of fresh air at the Frilandsmuseet*

dress up in, as well as Viking board games and drawing activities. Tycho Brahe Planetarium (page 82) is probably more suited to children than adults, particularly the IMAX shows. There are several other places which are guaranteed to keep younger visitors from being bored:

- **Guinness World of Records Museum** Lots of things to fascinate and horrify (in a gentle way). ⓐ Østergade 16. ⓣ 33 32 3131. ⓦ www.guinness.dk ⓛ Mon–Thur 10.00–22.30, Fri & Sat 10.00–18.00. Admission charge.

- **Ripley's Believe It or Not Museum** Another place to fascinate the young. ⓐ Rådhuspladsen. ⓣ 33 91 89 91. ⓦ www.ripleys.dk

- **Frilandsmuseet (Open-air Museum)** An outdoor museum of Danish rural life. Children can watch the demonstrations of dancing, take a ride in a horse carriage and see costumed farm workers handling the animals. Better at weekends for the demonstrations. ⓐ Kongevejen 100, Lyngby. ⓣ 33 13 44 11;. ⓦ www.natmus.dk ⓛ Tues–Sun 10.00–17.00. Admission charge for adult members of the party. ⓝ S-train Sorgenfri; bus 184 from Nørreport Station.

COMMUNICATIONS
Phones
Public telephones are either coin- or card-operated. The former take coins from 1kr to 20kr but do not give change. Cards can be bought at S-train stations and post offices. They come in denominations of 30, 50 and 100kr and work out slightly cheaper than using coins. A display in the phone box tells you how much credit you have left.

Calls are cheaper after 19.30. Directory enquiries is 118 and overseas directory enquiries is 113. The yellow pages is on the internet (ⓦ www.degulesider.dk).

The international dialling code for Denmark is 45. To dial any of the Danish numbers in this book from your own country, dial your own international access code (e.g. 00 for the UK), then 45, then the 8-digit number. All private phones in Denmark have 8 digits and there are no area codes.

To dial abroad from Denmark, dial 00 followed by your own country's international code (UK 44, Ireland 353, USA and Canada 1, Australia 61, New Zealand 64, South Africa 27) and then the area code (leaving off the first 0 in UK numbers) and number.

Post

Letters weighing up to 50g to destinations within Denmark are 4.50Kr. The same letter will cost 6Kr. to a European destination and 7Kr. to the rest of the world.

Main post office ⓐ Fisketorvet, ❶ 33 41 56 00. ◷ Mon–Fri 11.00–18.00, Sat 10.00–13.00. There is also a post office in Central Station, ◷ Mon–Fri 08.00–21.00, Sat 09.00–16.00, Sun 10.00–16.00.

Internet

Internet cafés are a rarity in Copenhagen, since everyone is wired up and doesn't need to use a café. Most hotels offer free internet connections to their guests and the more expensive places have internet access in the room. Public libraries have computers with internet access and should you need to download digital photographs these are the best places to seek out since internet cafés such as the one in Central Station do not have adequate

connections. Public libraries include:

Det Kongelige Bibliotek Søren Kierkegaards Plads.

Hovedbiblioteket Krystalgade 15.

ELECTRICITY

Denmark runs on 220V 50Hz AC. If the electrical equipment you are bringing – mobile phone, laptop, electric razor – doesn't run on these parameters you should obtain a special transformer for them, or consider doing without them. Danish sockets are round two-pin ones. Adapters are best bought in your home country, since Danish shops sell adapters for Danes going abroad rather than for visitors. Most hotels have square three-pin adapters you can borrow.

TRAVELLERS WITH DISABILITIES

Like most European cities Copenhagen builds new buildings and services with disabled people in mind. Buses have lowering ramps for wheelchairs and the newer hotels will have rooms which are adapted to use for handicapped people. Public toilets in newer buildings are disabled-friendly and the metro has lifts and easy-access carriages. Older buildings are less accessible. A free pamphlet is available from the tourist office which lists hotels, restaurants, museums and churches that are accessible to wheelchairs and have other facilities for disabled visitors.

In the city further help can be sought at Dansk Handicap Forbund. Kollektivhuset, Hans Knudsens Plads 1A. 39 29 35 55.

FURTHER INFORMATION

Tourist information

Copenhagen Right Now The main tourist information centre in Copenhagen with a café, shop, free internet access and helpful staff

who will book accommodation. Lots of free information and maps.
ⓐ Vesterbrogade 4A, København. ⓣ 70 22 24 42.
ⓦ www.visitcopenhagen.dk ⓛ Mon–Sat 09.00–18.00, May–Jun;
Mon–Sat 09.00–20.00, Sun 10.00–18.00 July–Aug; Mon–Fri
09.00–16.00, Sat 09.00–14.00 Sep–Apr.

Helsingør Tourist Office Useful maps of the town and
accommodation information. ⓐ Havnepladsen 3, Helsingør.
ⓣ 49 21 13 33. ⓦ www.visithelsingor.dk

Roskilde Tourist Office Maps, accommodation, free guide to the
town. ⓐ Gullandstrasse 15, Roskilde. ⓣ 46 31 65 65.
ⓦ www.visitroskilde.com

Background reading

Michael Booth *Just As well I'm Leaving*. Some humorous comments
on living among the Danes.
Peter Høeg *Miss Smilla's Feeling for Snow*. Almost supernatural crime
thriller set in Christianshavn.
Hans Christian Andersen *The Complete Fairy Tales*. Get in the mood
for the city with some very weird fairytales.
Michael Frayn *Copenhagen*. Strange play which discusses quantum
physics, loyalty and betrayal.
Karen Blixen *Seven Gothic Tales*. The Danish writer's take on the
gothic.
Christopher Woodward *The Buildings of Europe: Copenhagen*.
Illustrated guide to many of Copenhagen's architecturally
interesting buildings.
Stig Hornshøj-Møller *A Short History of Denmark*. Good, brief
account of several thousand years of history.

Useful phrases

Although English is spoken widely in Denmark, these words and pharses may come in handy. Note that r is often pronounced emphatically, shown as rr in the pronunciation guide.

English	Danish	Approx. pronunciation
BASICS		
Yes	Ja	Ya
No	Nej	Nai
Thank you	Tak	Tahg
Hello	Hej	Hai
Goodbye	Hej hej	Hai hai
Excuse me	Undskyld	Ornskewl
Sorry	Undskyld	Ornsgewl
That's okay	Det er i orden	Di ehrr ee orrdehn
To	Til	Ti
From	Fra	Frah
Do you speak English	Taler De engelsk?	Tala dee ehng-ehlsg?
Good morning	God morgen	Gor morn
Good afternoon	Got eftermiddag	Gor ehfdamidda
Good evening	Godaften	Gor-ahfdehn
Goodnight	Godnat	Goh-nad
My name is ...	Mit navn er ...	Mid nown ehr ...

English	Danish	Approx. pronunciation
DAYS & TIMES		
Monday	Mandag	manda
Tuesday	Tirsdag	teerrsda
Wednesday	Onsdag	ornsda
Thursday	Torsdag	torrsda
Friday	Fredag	Frrehdag
Saturday	Lørdag	Lerda
Sunday	Søndag	Sernda
Morning	Morgen	Morn
Afternoon	Eftermiddag	Ehfdahmidda
Night	Nad	Nat
Yesterday	I gå	Ee gor

English	Danish	*Approx. pronunciation*
Today	I dag	*Ee dag*
Tomorrow	I morgen	*Ee morn*
What time is it?	Hvad er klokken?	*Va ehrr kloggehn?*
It is ...	Klokken er ...	*Kloggehn ehr ...*
09.00	Ni om morgenen	*Nee om morrnen*
Midday	Middagstid	*Midahsteeth*
Midnight	Midnat	*Meethnad*

NUMBERS

One	En	*In*
Two	To	*Tor*
Three	Tre	*Trreh*
Four	Fire	*Feerr*
Five	Fem	*Feh*
Six	Seks	*Sehgs*
Seven	Syv	*Suw*
Eight	Otte	*Ordeh*
Nine	Ni	*Nee*
Ten	Ti	*Tee*
Eleven	Elve	*Ehlveh*
Twelve	Tolv	*Tol*
Twenty	Tyve	*Tuw-weh*
Fifty	Halvtreds	*Haltrrehs*
One hundred	Hundrede	*Hoonahth*

MONEY

I would like to change these traveller's cheques/this currency	Jeg vil gerne veksle rejsechecks/penge	*Yai vi gehrrneh vehgsleh Rraisseh-shehgs/pehngeh*
Do you accept credit cards?	Tager I kreditkort?	*Tah ee krehdeedkord?*

SIGNS & NOTICES

Airport	Lufthavn
Rail station/Platform	Togstation/Perron
Smoking/non-smoking	Rygning/Rygning Forbudt
Toilets	Toilet
Open/Closed	Åben/Lukket

Emergencies

EMERGENCY NUMBERS
Police, ambulance or fire service 112

Missing credit cards 24-hour service ☎ 44 89 29 29. You can also report lost or stolen cards to Amex ☎ 70 20 70 97; Diners Club ☎ 36 73 73 73; Mastercard, Eurocard, Access ☎ 80 01 60 98; Visa ☎ 80 01 85 88.

Lost Property on buses ☎ 36 13 14 15

MEDICAL EMERGENCIES
Doctor
Your hotel will have a list of local doctors and the tourist office has the number of a doctor on call through the night: ☎ 70 13 00 41, 16.00–08.00.
Between 08.00–16.00 Mon–Fri you can call ☎ 33 93.63.00 and give your location to be given the address of a doctor near you. Outside these hours call ☎ 38 88 60 41.
Doctor's fees are around 250Kr. plus and must be paid in cash. Keep receipts if you want to make an insurance claim.
City General Practice & Travel Medicine ⓐ Ny Østergad.
☎ 70 27 57 57

Dentist
In a dental emergency the tourist office can recommend a dentist. Dentists' fees are paid in cash.
Emergency dental service ⓐ Oslo Plads 14. ☎ 36 38.02.51. 08.00–21.30 Mon–Fri, 10.00–12.00 Sat, Sun.

Hospitals

24 hour accident and emergency departments can be found at:

Amager Hospital 🖂 Italiensvej 1, Amager. ☎ 32 34 32 34.
Bispebjerg Hospital 🖂 Bispebjerg Bakke 23. ☎ 35 31 35 31
Frederiksberg Hospital 🖂 Nordre Fasanvej 57, Frederiksberg.
☎ 38 16 38 16.

Pharmacies

Most pharmacies keep general shopping hours. You can recognise
them from the sign Apotek above the door.

Steno Apotek Opposite Central Station and open 24 hours.
🖂 Vesterbogade 6. ☎ 33 14 82 66.

Police Stations

🖂 Halmtorvet 20. ☎ 33 25 14 48.
🖂 Store Kongesgade 100. ☎ 33 93 14 48.

EMERGENCY PHRASES

Help!
Hjælp!
Yehlb!

Can you help me?
Kan De hjæpe mig?
Ka Dee yehlbeh mai?

Call an ambulance/a doctor/the police!
Ring efter en ambulance/en læge/politiet!
Ring ehfda in ahmboolahnseh/in leh-eh/porlitee-eht!

EMBASSIES & CONSULATES

In an emergency such as theft or injury your country's embassy will expect you to go through the emergency procedures in Copenhagen. They will also expect you to have taken out travel insurance which will cover your needs. If the emergency is of your own making, such as an arrest for drunk driving or disorderly conduct, you will again be subject to the laws of Denmark and the embassy will be unable to intervene. Embassies can, however, issue a replacement passport. The following is a list of embassies in Copenhagen:

Australian @ Dampfærgevej 26. ✆ 70 26 36 76.
Ⓦ www.denmarkembassy.gov.au
British @ Kastelsvej 40. ✆ 35 44 52 00. Ⓦ www.britishembassy.dk
Canadian @ Kristen Bernikows Gade 1. ✆ 33 48. 32 00.
Ⓦ www.dfait-maeci.gc.ca/canadaeuropa/denmark/
Irish @ Østbanegade 21. ✆ 35 42 32 33.
US @ Dag Hammarskjölds Allé 24. ✆ 35 55 31 44.
Ⓦ www.usembassy.dk

▶ *Copenhagen is safe and easy to get around*

The publishers would like to thank the following individuals and organisations for supplying their copyright photographs for this book.
A1 Pix: pages 40, 59 and 65.
Hotel Alexandra: page 36.
Radisson SAS Royal Hotel: page 39.
Salt Bar/Restaurant: pages 25 and 75.
Visit Copenhagen: pages 31, 115 and 147.
Visit Denmark: pages 1, 13, 21, 62, 79, 81, 112, 127, 128, 135 and 139.
Pat Levy: all other pages.

Proofreader: Angela Chevalier-Watts
Copy-editor: Stephen York

Send your thoughts to
books@thomascook.com

- **Found a great bar, club, shop or must-see sight that we don't feature?**

- **Like to tip us off about any information that needs a little updating?**

- **Want to tell us what you love about this handy little guidebook and more importantly how we can make it even handier?**

Then here's your chance to tell all! Send us ideas, discoveries and recommendations today and then look out for your valuable input in the next edition of this title. As an extra 'thank you' from Thomas Cook Publishing, you'll be automatically entered into our exciting monthly prize draw.

Email the above address (stating the book's title) or write to: CitySpots Project Editor, Thomas Cook Publishing, PO Box 227, Unit 15/16, Coningsby Road, Peterborough PE3 8SB, UK.